Dr. Cott's Help for Your Learning Disabled Child

Dr. Cott's Help for Your Learning Disabled Child

The Orthomolecular Treatment

by Allan Cott, M.D.

with Jerome Agel
and Eugene Boe

Copyright © 1985 by Jerome Agel

All rights reserved under International and Pan-American
Copyright Conventions. Published in the United States by Times
Books, a division of Random House, Inc., New York, and
simultaneously in Canada by Random House of Canada Limited,
Toronto.

Library of Congress Cataloging in Publication Data

Cott, Allan, 1910–
    Dr. Cott's help for your learning disabled child.

    Bibliography: p. 239
    Includes index.
    1. Learning disabilities—Diet therapy.   2. Ortho-
molecular therapy.   I. Agel, Jerome.   II. Boe, Eugene.
III. Title.   IV. Title: Help for your learning disabled child.
RJ496.L4C68   1985   618.92'89   84-40417
ISBN 0-8129-1147-4

Designed by Doris Borowsky

Manufactured in the United States of America

9 8 7 6 5 4 3 2 1

First Edition

TABLE OF CONTENTS

Note

The ideas, procedures, and suggestions put forward in this book are not intended as a substitute for consultation with your physician. *All* matters regarding your child's health require medical supervision.

Dr. Cott's
Help for Your
Learning Disabled
Child

"*Agony is given in strange ways to children.*"

—*Flannery O'Connor*

"*Let nothing that can be treated by diet be treated by other means.*"

—*Maimonides (1135–1204)*

Chapter I

There's Hope—and Real Help

YOU KNOW THIS child. Or one quite similar to him. He may even be *your* child.

"He's climbing the walls, Dr. Cott."

"He can't sit still."

"He can't concentrate."

"She's failing in school when she should be at the head of the class."

"He keeps everyone in the house up all night."

"He's flying apart, Dr. Cott."

These typically are the lamentations of parents with hyperactive children. The offshoot of hyperactivity is the inability to learn optimally. Children with learning and behavioral disabilities fall into a gray area between the sunshine of normalcy and the darkness of severe mental disorders. These children—and they number in the millions—are our shadow children.

Too often, handicapped children such as these go undiagnosed and pass for normal children. This is why we say the shadow child is afflicted with an "invisible handicap."

A learning disability is a disorder in one or more of the basic psychological processes involved in understanding or in using language—spoken or written—which may manifest itself in an imperfect ability to listen, think, speak, read, write, spell, or do mathematical calculations. These disabilities include such conditions as perceptual handicaps, dyslexia, and developmental aphasia (partial or total loss of speech or loss of understanding of language). But they do not include mental retardation or problems that are primarily the result of visual, hearing, or motor handicaps.

Learning disabilities constitute the most prevalent and urgent medical problem of children in the developed countries of the world. In the United States alone there may be 10 million children, or more, whose learning functions are impaired and whose disorders range from mild to thoroughly incapacitating. A high percentage of these youngsters have the specific disorder of dyslexia. For reasons that can only be speculated upon, a high proportion of learning disabled children (perhaps four out of five) is male.

If not corrected, these disorders will be lifelong. Many of these disadvantaged young people, as they enter adolescence, will take to drink or drugs and become juvenile delinquents. Many will go on to a career of crime. They will enter the vocational world with lower educational achievements and lacking occupational skills. Their antisocial or withdrawn behavior will make them prone to job dismissals, social rejection, and accidents. More likely, they will be drawing a welfare check rather than a paycheck. Learning disabled children who are not helped grow up to become handicapped adults. Learning disabled children do not outgrow their handicap, only their clothes.

Most parents, in my initial consultation with them, admit that they missed the early presumptive signs of a child at risk for learning disabilities. The decision to bring their child for

4

help comes when they begin to understand that the energy that the child is exerting is not coming from the normal exuberance of childhood but from a source that is driving him relentlessly and that is *not within his control.*

"Like a rocket jetting through the universe, he hurtles through life," one mother has described her shadow child. "He is an attractive child. He smiles a lot. He has freckles on his cheeks and nose, and his eyes shine with excitement. Yet I wonder if he notices the expressions of the people around him as he propels himself into a room where company is seated. Does he see the looks on their faces turn to facades of controlled composure? Does he see their hands curl with tension around the arms of their chairs . . . ?"

I would be the first to say that many learning impaired children are enormously appealing. They can exude a charm, a sweetness, and a kindness far exceeding that of average children. They can be almost clairvoyant in sensing that something is bothering an adult, and they will perform some impulsive, compassionate gesture by way of giving solace. How friendly and outgoing they can be! Just don't expect them to remember who you are the next time they see you.

Many of these children have a cleverness and an intelligence that almost camouflage their learning problems. Some will go to extraordinary lengths to compensate for their learning deficits and to discourage the notion that they are having any academic difficulties. In order to keep up with their classmates they will develop some kind of excellence within their capabilities. With a strong ego and a considerable persistence, these children may seem to be "getting by." Stymied by a reading difficulty, a child may develop extraordinary powers of memory that will enable him to process and to retain information acquired by listening. But learning circuits remain crossed, nonetheless. Only with superhuman effort can a learning disabled child meet

5

the challenge to excel. Though it's rare, it does happen. The roster of the learning disabled includes such illustrious names as Sir Winston Churchill, Albert Einstein, Hans Christian Andersen, Thomas Edison, August Rodin, W. B. Yeats, Dr. Harvey Cushing, Vice President Nelson A. Rockefeller (who once "wrote" a book he couldn't read), General George Patton, Jr., and Gustave Flaubert.

When worried parents call for an appointment to bring their child in to see me, I routinely ask how they learned of my work. Variously, I hear:

"I was referred to you by my pediatrician."

"I read that newspaper interview with you, the one in which you talked about how good nutrition affects the brain. That makes a lot of sense to me."

"I am fed up with having my child drugged to make him 'manageable.'"

"I've seen how you've helped my neighbor's daughter, and maybe you can do the same for my child."

"We've tried everything else; nothing has worked."

These parents indeed feel hopeless and helpless. Most of them have tried every other therapeutic approach without discernible results. Nothing worked—or worked in any dynamic way.

From my own experience, I am peculiarly able to appreciate the frustration of these parents and their intelligent but disordered children. It took me a long time to arrive at the techniques that I have been using successfully to treat the learning disabled for the past twenty-five years. For many years prior to that, I was a conventional fifty-minute-hour psychiatrist struggling to "analyze" away the anguish of my patients. This was a particularly ineffective approach with children who were having so many basic problems with communication itself. Always nutritionally oriented, I became convinced from the empirical evidence that the learning and behavioral disorders of most children could be traced to a biochemical imbalance in the brain. Correct this imbalance and we would be well on the way to resolving the problems of these children.

The primary goal of my orthomolecular approach is to straighten out ("ortho" literally means "straight") the disoriented biochemistry in the brain. The treatment combines larger than Recommended Daily Allowance dosages of vitamin and mineral supplements with drastic dietary reforms. On this regimen, thousands upon thousands of shadow children have at last become susceptible to learning, and to learning in serenity.

"Dr. Cott," a mother will ask me on the telephone, "when may I bring Richard in for consultation?"

"Before you come in," I advise her, "there are certain things I want you to do. I am sending you a comprehensive questionnaire, and I would like you to answer everything as best you can. I also want your son to have some routine blood tests and an analysis of both the nutrient and the toxic minerals. A test of his hair will give us this analysis."

"A hair test? Why?"

"Because hair reflects tissue levels of the nutrients."

"Where can it be done?"

"Any laboratory that has the approval of the Center for Disease Control."

At some point, there is usually a hesitation on the other end of the phone. I can anticipate what the caller would like to ask: Is the orthomolecular approach going to work for her child? What are the chances that he or she will really get well?

"The chances are fifty percent or better," I can tell the parent.

A conservative answer, to be sure, but I go on to explain, "Fifty percent or better if you see to it that your child faithfully adheres to the strictures of the program. The chances are lessened if you are not stringent in your control of his diet and in making sure that the substances I prescribe are taken in the proper doses. Some children are not reachable by *any* treatment. There are still factors in brain function that we do not know about. But as I say, the chances are excellent that your child will improve greatly by the orthomolecular approach if you follow the rules."

I caution parents that it could take up to two or three years to achieve the maximum results. At the end of treatment, a proud mother will usually bring her recovered child in to see me.

"Do you remember what Richard was like when I brought him in that first time, Dr. Cott?"

Remember? How could I forget! A child racing around the office like a bullet train, bowling over chairs like duckpins, banging his head on my desk, yelling and screaming, answering my questions like a tape recorder on fast rewind.

"Look at him now," his mother says, beaming.

I see a child who is transformed. He can sit still. He can concentrate. He can communicate intelligently. He reads and writes easily. He smiles and talks enthusiastically about school and new friends. His grooming is vastly improved.

I see a child who has been rescued from his own miseries and who no longer makes those around him miserable.

I see a child who has joined the world as a sociable, adaptable, *learning* person.

Yes, the orthomolecular approach to learning and behavioral difficulties works!

This book is a commemoration of my commitment to the use of orthomolecular medicine in leading our shadow children out of the darkness and into their own place in the sun.

Chapter II

Facing Facts—and Taking Action

THERE IS NO such thing as a completely "normal" child, nor are any two children quite identical. No human being is a carbon copy of any other; each child has the uniqueness of a snowflake and is, biochemically, separate and individual. To describe a child as normal or "different" is merely to apply a convenient label to infinitely complex abstractions.

Those children who are somewhere between the child who is well and functioning and the child who is very ill and functioning minimally fall into a no-man's land, a gray area—thus the designation shadow children.

The nature of their problems is subtle. These children neither do well in the world of the normal, nor are they in need of the special treatment appropriate to the abnormal. If untreated, they are doomed to live in a world whose expectations they cannot meet through any fault of their own. To function on a level with that of their peer age group is beyond the range of their capabilities. Too many of them must cope as best they can without any understanding of the depths of their difficulties from their parents, siblings, peers, or teachers.

DR. COTT'S HELP FOR YOUR LEARNING DISABLED CHILD

In the learning disabled children I treat, I perceive an acute, aching loneliness. These are children in isolation, unable to grasp the cause of their isolation. Little wonder that they have so many outbursts and temper tantrums or that they turn to compensatory behavior. Many have a tendency to bossiness. Because they are "backward" students and must show muscle elsewhere, some will boast to me that they were the first in their circle to use marijuana.

School dropouts claim they have better things to do than "being caged up" in a classroom all day. If getting into drugs and other criminal activities is the cost of attracting attention or being acceptable to an antisocial peer group, they will pay it. The youngster who decides he is better off out of school has embarked on a life-style that eases the unbearable tension and anxiety he encountered every day in the schoolhouse "prison." Failures in school become cumulative. At some point, the frustrated child ceases to yearn, to strive. His behavior worsens and the punishments increase. The school either ignores or expels him and he becomes one more dropout. Expulsion from school, dropping out, or even truancy leads to delinquency. Delinquent children are often the underachievers who, in the beginning, never learned to read or write—not because they did not want to learn but because they *couldn't*.

Each year, hundreds of thousands of school dropouts join the millions who preceded them, becoming part of the ever-expanding army of idlers who roam our streets. It is hardly surprising that 75 percent of the truants in New York City are illiterate. The Bureau of Prisons informs us that an overwhelming majority of the inmates of the nation's jails are either totally or functionally illiterate. To "make a living," most had little choice but to resort to a life of crime. (Iceland has 100 percent literacy and no prisons. It didn't experience an armed robbery until 1984.)

Social and intellectual maturation proceeds a day at a time.

But the learning disabled child does not make increments of progress. He lags behind his classmates, and in the cruelty and candor common to children he is dismissed and belittled with comments such as, "He still talks funny"; "He's nine years old and can't tie his shoelaces"; "She can't remember her own phone number."

In describing their learning disabled children, mothers are describing children who are trying to thread a needle while wearing mittens. " 'I won't do it,' " I point out, "is your child's prideful way of saying, 'I can't do it, Mom, I *can't* do it.' "

Too often, parents, many of them in tears, cannot comprehend the complexity of their children's problems. They will say to me:

"Why can't he get it through his head that it is *c-a-t* and not *t-a-c-?*"

"Why does he pick up the ball when I ask him to pick up the bowl?"

"Overnight, he forgets everything he learned yesterday."

"He can discuss the mathematical possibilities of extraterrestrial life but can't add two and two."

"Try as I do, I can't drum into him the difference between *b* and *d* or the days of the week in the right order."

"His teacher tells me that he is a holy terror in the classroom."

"How is it possible that such an angelic-looking child can be so monstrously destructive?"

These "monstrously destructive" children could drive anyone to tears when they say *"I won't do it"* a hundred times a day or more.

Thorough as is my questionnaire, I can arrive at only an approximate profile of the child. Uniqueness implies that there will always be unknown and undetectable components in the personalities of these children as well as for everyone else.

I make a special effort to be comforting to vexed and usually guilt-ridden parents. "It is not because you haven't tried," I tell them. "It is not that your child is inherently stubborn or dull. Or lazy. Or perverse. Or mean. Or spoiled. I know how difficult it is for you to accept the fact that your child has a serious underlying problem. He looks as normal as Jack Armstrong and he is as smart as any of the other kids on the block. But please try to accept this: He has a problem that interferes with his making progress on several fronts."

From my practice, I find that it is especially difficult for parents to recognize the early signs of a learning impaired child if he is their firstborn. Only when there is a second child who behaves "normally" do they have a basis for comparison. When their overactive infant pulls himself to his feet at six months, climbs out of the crib at eight months, and is walking at nine months and running at ten months, the parents tend to be pleased. They even boast of his precociousness. Pride turns to dismay when the child plunges into a maelstrom of hyperactivity, which is so often—but by no means always—the harbinger of a learning dysfunction.

Strange as it may seem, many parents do not even recognize hyperactivity as such when they see it. Their child may be destroying everything in his path and rushing frenetically from one activity to the next. He may not be able to sleep or concentrate or display even one iota of visual or muscular coordination. Yet all of these telltale symptoms will be lumped together and minimized as "just a phase he's passing through."

A parent's first question, in facing the facts, will be, "Dr. Cott, what caused this?"

"It could be one of any number of causes," I respond. "There is no easy answer."

I try to generalize rather than speculate in their particular instance, and I make a point not to get too technical. I prefer not to speak of "maturational imbalances" or "developmental or neurological or organic impairments" or "discrepancies between expectant potential and actual performance" or even of "deficits in the intellectual, sensory, emotional, or environmental areas." I do explain that the origin of the child's difficulties may be genetic, or inherited. The brain may not be functioning properly even though it is not damaged; the problem is a dysfunction in the chemistry of the brain. We use the term minimal brain dysfunction (MBD) to refer to certain learning or behavioral disabilities in children of near or above average intelligence; these disabilities range from mild to severe, and are associated with deviations of function of the central nervous system. If there is a brain malfunction, I point out, it is rarely the result of physical damage to the brain.

Finally, and here I do not mince my words, I tell parents that many children get off to a bad start because their mothers have neglected or mistreated themselves during pregnancy. (I shall be discussing this key factor in Chapter XI, "Coming into the World.")

Many shadow children are the victims of an erroneous diagnosis. They are written off as dense or even mentally retarded, but they are not. Many children are given life sentences in institutions, but they do not belong there. There are thousands of "behavioral problems" and "slow learners" in residential facilities for the retarded, and they do not belong there, either. There are children who have learning problems without being learning disabled; these children are at the bottom of the normal range of mental development; they may have IQs of 90 or thereabouts, so they are neither retarded nor learning disabled.

So familiar today is the term "learning disabilities," it is hard to believe that it did not enter our language until the 1960s. But it merely describes a syndrome, not a specific child with specific problems. It classifies children but does not help to teach them. These children are alternately described as minimally brain damaged, educationally handicapped, neurologically immature, hyperkinetic, perceptually handicapped, maturationally lagging, attention deficited, and by more than forty other terms.

Learning disabilities are not disorders like the usual childhood diseases with which all parents are familiar. The signs that characterize this dysfunction occur in groups or clusters; symptoms will often vary, just as children vary in other respects. Some children have difficulty in reading, because they have trouble distinguishing letters that look alike—or they have word reversals in which the sequence of letters appears to them in reverse of the word on the printed page or blackboard. Many children who frequently rub their eyes have disturbances in the important visual functions so necessary to reading. The eyes of visually impaired children may not move smoothly over the printed line because they lack smooth muscle control; if focusing is not properly established, these children may skip words in the line, lose their place, and be unable to comprehend what they read.

Problems of this nature can often be spotted by observing a child's posture as he reads or writes, for he will often cock his head at a sharp angle and lower it until it is only inches away from the page he's trying to read. Frequently, the child is unable to follow successive words in reading unless he moves his finger along the page under each word.

Some children reveal visual-motor or perceptual-motor problems that prevent their hands or feet from processing the information their eyes give them. These children will not perform well in sports, because it takes coordination to catch a ball, to bat, to kick, or to throw with some degree of accuracy. This lack of "follow-through" in their large muscles makes their movements clumsy. They, therefore, tend to avoid sports and to show interest in solitary activities rather than subject themselves to the possible ridicule of their peers.

Other children lack fine-finger control; if they are coloring, they cannot keep within the outlines of the drawing they are coloring. Because they cannot hold a pencil in a proper pincer grip, their writing is awkward; letters are written above or below the line, some very small, others gigantic by comparison. Lack of finger control will also manifest itself early in a child's inability to cut with scissors.

The characteristic sign most often observed among learning disabled children is hyperactivity. But not all children with disorders of learning, behavior, and communication are hyperactive. Hyperactivity is recognizable by such manifestations as rambunctiousness, the inability to sit still or concentrate, short attention span, and disturbed sleeping patterns.

I can say categorically that learning problems rarely occur in isolated form. If a child is having difficulty in one area, he is almost certainly going to have difficulty in another. I have seldom seen a dyslexic child, for example, who did not also have dyscalcula (difficulty with mathematics), dysgraphia (difficulty with writing), and other learning problems.

The child who cannot perform on a level with his peers is a child who will in one way or another be destroyed and never achieve his full potential. He is improperly assessed by his parents, his teachers, and his classmates. Other children may ultimately destroy the fragile threads of the self-esteem he strives to maintain when they label him a "retard." By and by, he is precipitated into an emotional disorder as he progresses through each school year under the mounting stress of demands to perform beyond his capabilities. Early recognition of his difficulties can help avoid disaster by prompt intervention into his problems.

As the parents begin to accept the fact that they have a

learning disabled child, I say to them with emphasis, "And please remember, the primary responsibility for treatment and for your child's improvement must rest with you. You cannot expect too much from teachers or the schools. They are already overburdened with the loads they have to carry. They don't have the resources for children with special requirements."

From the thousands of parents who have come to me for help, I can sketch a composite profile of parental pain, resignation, cooperation, and optimism.

"There is nothing really wrong with my child," a parent will still protest. "He only needs more time and understanding" (or a better teacher or a better school).

"I honestly think it was that psychologist we took him to who caused all the problems" goes a familiar evasion. "He certainly did more harm than good."

"Can you explain to me, Dr. Cott, why everyone treats Andy so terribly? So he's a little slow and awkward. But he has many fine points, don't you agree?"

Guilt finds expression: "Where did we go wrong? Did we give him too loose a rein? Was it because we wouldn't let him be inoculated?"

There is also righteous indignation: "With all those specialists coming through the school and testing this and that, you'd think they could see he had a problem. Why did those teachers pass him from one grade to the next if he was failing?"

There is a lot of familial anger, anger between the parents and at their child: "It's all your fault for overindulging him and thinking everything he does is so cute." Or "If there *is* something wrong with him, it comes from your side of the family." Or "I shouldn't say this, but there are times when that kid gets me so riled up I could choke him."

There is fear, quaking fear: "We've had him so many places and nothing has worked. Do you really think, Dr. Cott, your method will do him any good?"

Fear gives way to a measure of self-pity and injustice-collecting: "What did we do to deserve this?" "No other child had a better home." "You really try to do your best and then *this* happens."

Then comes what I call employing the "what if?" tactic: "What if we should move to another neighborhood?" "What if we find a more progressive school?" "What if we send him to a special camp this summer?" "What if we take the television set out of the house and have three hours of enforced homework every night?"

Finally, after we have worked through this litany of emotions—and the spells of despair and depression—there is acceptance and the dawn of hope. Yes, of course the child has a problem. Yes, deep down in their hearts parents know the orthomolecular approach makes sense. Now at last they are on to something that *can* succeed and give a new life to their shadow child.

Chapter III

There Had to Be a Better Way

WHEN I BEGAN my medical training, little attention was being given to the biochemistry of the brain. All psychotic and neurotic behavior was thought to be rooted exclusively in bad parenting. To help a disturbed patient, the psychiatrist had only to "work through" with him the primary sources of his disorder—namely, Mommy and Daddy. The patient talked, talked, talked, and doctor and patient alike were persuaded that only out of the painful remembrance of things past could the demons be exorcised. This was the classic psychotherapeutic approach.

For years, as a traditional psychiatrist, I, too, sat either behind or at the side of a couch for ten hours every day. These interminable sessions yielded only variations on the themes of pain and disorientation. Eventually, I couldn't help but question a premise whose results were so discouraging. What was being accomplished by all the talking and all the listening? There were just too many distraught patients whose emotional problems could not be laid at the doorstep of abusive or negligent parents. Large numbers, especially of the young, were not reachable through Freudian techniques. I concluded that psychoanalysis was a discipline as endless as it was frustrating.

This disenchantment with classical therapy took a certain amount of fortitude. After all, my training had been decades in the making: twenty years of academic education, two years of general internship, four years of specialty training, and three years of overseas military service as a psychiatrist and acting psychiatric consultant for the Persian Gulf Command of the Army. Nor did I see any other pragmatic, rational approach to treatment at hand. (This was about the time when LSD was being hailed as the "miracle worker" that would plumb the potential of the human mind and resolve its vagaries and torments. But any sustained use of LSD was unthinkable.)

Because of this disillusionment with traditional therapy, I knew I had to find a more dynamic method of treatment than the interplay of words between patient and doctor. The fifty-minute hours were not geared to helping children who were severely disordered or who had the milder affliction of a learning disability. These children, with their deficits in attention, problems with communication, and hyperkinetic behavior, needed some dramatic form of intervention to subdue their inner tornado. Only after they were becalmed could they become accessible either to remedial learning or to professional counseling.

Parents of learning disabled children routinely seek the counsel of the family physician. But the general practitioner, however well-meaning, is ineffectual in treating learning or behavioral impairments. The standard accoutrements of stethoscopes, reflex hammers, and homely homilies do not disentangle the scrambled circuits of these specifically disordered youngsters.

Nor do I find the behavioral approach favored by many child psychologists a satisfactory way of getting at the roots of the

problems of the learning disabled child. This method empha-
sizes deliberate control of the life of the child and his family
in order to provide the maximum in positive experiences for
the child and for those around him. I think this is all to the
good as a useful adjunctive or alternative therapy. It is certainly
helpful that daily goals be tailored for this child and that he
be praised if he achieves them. But progress at home and at
school and in behavioral and learning goals cannot be altogether
manipulated; something has to be at work moving from the
interior to the surface.

So commonplace have these disabilities become that we now
have expanding battalions of "experts" specializing in "problem
children." We have friends and neighbors eager to help by
sharing their experiences with a child who went through "just
what your Danny is going through now." I have always advised
parents that someone else's Johnny is not their Danny. Misery
may love company, but amateur group therapy is not very
productive.

But it is drugs to this day that remain the primary intervention in the treatment of learning disabled children. Admittedly, drugs do subdue a child whose hyperactivity is interfering with his learning. They make his presence and
deportment more welcome in the classroom. But they, too,
are not getting at the heart of the matter. There is the rationale
that the child is underaroused and is in need of stimulation to
process information; ergo, stimulant drugs are administered
to correct the child's attention deficit. Stimulant drugs, par-
adoxically, have a quite different effect on hyperactive children
than they do on adults or even on other children; they calm
and soothe—and theoretically render more educable—rather
than fire up and hyperactivate.

Superficially, the child treated with drugs will seem to be
paying attention, but the question is how much is being truly

digested. Any observable gains will be more apparent than real unless they are complemented by a fundamental approach to the child's difficulties.

The child's state of passivity and compliance induced by the drug is interpreted as a benefit to him. He becomes "nicer," and we tend to think of nice children as those who are obedient and do their lessons. But should we be sacrificing spontaneity and expressiveness on the altar of good deportment? Should we be using medications to enforce debatable societal norms on bright children whose underlying learning problems, not surface rambunctiousness, are the real issue?

However one may feel about treatment with drugs, in some situations I believe they should be considered for short-term use. If the child's disruptive behavior prevents the others in the classroom from learning, the options offered to the parents are to consider the use of drugs for a period of time or to remove the child from the school and find a specialized school whose tuition may be prohibitive.

But the promiscuous use of medications is rightly raising considerable alarm. A special conference called by the Department of Health, Education, and Welfare posed the question of whether, in the first place, these drugs are safe for children. Are they being administered mainly as a disciplinary crutch? Where, in the long run, were children headed on a regimen of amphetamines or tranquilizers?

Without making any claims for prescience, I could have predicted the conclusions of the HEW panel:

- Appearances of academic improvement notwithstanding, *these medications are no panacea for a child's learning problems.*

- Under no circumstances should parents be coerced into permitting the administration of drugs.

- It is not the role of school personnel to prescribe treatment.

Furthermore, it is my belief that pharmaceutical companies manufacturing medications for the hyperkinetic disorders of children have a serious obligation. These products should be promoted ethically and made available only through medical channels. It should not be within the purview of school personnel to be recommending them. These drugs may control impulsive and distracting behavior, but they can also turn children into submissive, zombie-like creatures. Depression and withdrawal are frequent side effects, and so in the end, for many children, the drugs defeat the very purpose for which they are prescribed—to give the child the tranquillity and the eagerness to learn.

Just as much to the point: One-third to one-half of learning disabled children are *not helped at all*, even temporarily, by treatment with drugs. There is also no discernible, long-term effect even on a responding child's performance in school. A quieted youngster in the fourth grade with only a first-grade reading ability will still be unable to cope with a fourth-grade reading text. There is the factor of the continuing expense; prescribed medications are expensive. Far more serious is the fact of the severity of some of the side effects. Amphetamines induce loss of appetite. For children, this means not only weight loss but also a slowed rate of growth. Symptomatically, there are the accelerated heartbeats, elevated blood pressure, irritability, tearfulness, and ultimately sluggishness and fatigue. (Sweden and Japan, I understand, have banned the use of drugs to treat children who have learning problems, certainly a wise measure for any long-range approach to treatment.)

There is a subtler, long-range danger, too. A child who even thinks he is performing better in school may conclude that there must be a chemical solution for all of life's problems. I say unequivocally: *Drugs resolve no learning problems; they only disguise symptoms temporarily*.

Prescriptions for drugs come too easily. A doctor entrusted with the care of a learning disabled child should be prescribing nothing until he has obtained a complete history of the child. He will need to know how the youngster relates to family, teachers, and peers. Were the mother's pregnancy and the birth normal? What was the child's state of health during infancy and early childhood? What oddities of behavior has he displayed? What is he eating and drinking? Does he crave certain foods and beverages? What is the child's learning potential?

The direction that I was to move in was augured by my awareness of the extraordinary results that two research physicians in Canada were achieving with adult schizophrenics. Drs. Abram Hoffer and Humphry Osmond were pioneering in daring new pathways involving the use of vitamins. They were using massive dosages of certain vitamins in the treatment of these seriously ill patients, and the patients were responding wondrously.

When Dr. Osmond established the Bureau of Research in Neurology and Psychiatry at the New Jersey Neuro-Psychiatric Institute, in Princeton, I met with him and came away even more impressed with the techniques he was employing. I made the decision that I would initiate the orthomolecular approach in the treatment of my own very sick patients.

It would be hard to describe how gratifying I found the new methodology. How wonderful to see improvement before my very eyes, to be able to measure progress! Now, at last, I felt I was a doctor who was really helping and healing.

My particular area of specialization had its genesis in a phone call I received in the 1960s.

"Dr. Cott, I am aware of your work with adult schizophrenics," a distraught woman informed me. "I have a four-year-old son who has been diagnosed as a childhood schizophrenic. I have taken him everywhere, but nothing is helping. The last doctor we had put him on psychotropic drugs and it only made him worse. May I bring him to you for examination?"

I said yes, a little hesitantly; until then, all orthomolecular work had been exclusively with adult schizophrenics.

Mark was intensely hyperactive and engaging in frenetic ritualistic behavior and self-mutilation. He comprehended language but was unable to speak or exercise judgment or control. He screamed all day long without apparent provocation. He ran aimlessly around the house, breaking and battering things and causing such havoc that he had to be restricted to one room to prevent total mayhem—a room his parents referred to as "the bull pen."

The depth of the child's psychosis presented a challenge. He couldn't get much worse, and the vitamins and the minerals were certainly not going to harm him. I began treatment cautiously. I introduced one vitamin at a time. I added a new vitamin only after the dosage of the preceding one had been increased to the therapeutic level. Frequently, he refused to take the vitamins, and so his mother had to find a quite ingenious way of resolving the problem, and she did. She sat on him.

At no point did Mark experience side effects from the treatment. Quite the contrary. Within a few weeks, he was showing notable improvement. In less than three months, his screaming had stopped, his sleeping pattern had improved, and much of the hyperactivity had subsided. He began to speak . . . a word now and again. Somewhat later, he spoke in couplets and was demonstrating an increasing facility with vocabulary.

This was indeed an auspicious beginning for my work with seriously disturbed children. In the years following, parents by the hundreds brought their children to me for treatment with this method. The history of most of these children was that they had been treated with drugs and they had neither shown improvement nor gained much relief from their misery. Usually, schizophrenic and autistic children have an adverse reaction to drugs; their hyperactivity and otherwise disturbed behavior increase.

Some parents brought their children to me out of "last resort" desperation. Others began seeking this treatment as the first or primary means for coping with their children's schizophrenia, autism, or Down's syndrome. With faithful adherence to the program, my young patients improved and the symptoms of their psychotic behavior diminished; many of them became so tractable that they were able to enter into mainstream schooling.

No approach to the treatment of severe illnesses—or even to minimal brain dysfunction—can claim anything approaching a 100 percent record of success. This is hardly surprising. I have spoken of the uniqueness of every child, and every troubled child has a pattern of disorders unique to himself. Only after the thorough examination that I recommend can a program be designed to meet the child's specific needs. That child then will require constant observation and attention—primarily parental—if he is to make steady progress toward overcoming his handicap and achieving his potential.

After considerable experience with very sick boys and girls, I began to treat children who were less seriously disturbed. These were the learning disabled children who had such symptoms as intense hyperactivity, perceptual motor impairment, disruptive behavior in the classroom, general coordination deficits, inability to concentrate, short attention span, and frequently marginal disorders of speech. These were the children whose difficulties were not so conspicuous until they began to fall back in their studies.

Severe mental disorders and the milder learning disabilities are more complex than any of the usual malaises, such as measles, chicken pox, or mumps, that afflict children. I tend to avoid using the word *cure* in describing my work with young patients. But in my own judgment, I regard a child as "cured" when he begins to function behaviorally within acceptable bounds for someone his age and when he has become susceptible to the learning process. The time required for this adaptation varies according to the severity of each child's difficulties, his intelligence and emotional makeup, the involvement of the family, the age at which the disorder is detected, and the effectiveness of treatment. Early diagnosis and intervention accelerate improvement.

The orthomolecular treatment, as I came to practice it, embraced more than the administration of large dosages of vitamins and minerals. Early on, I began to place paramount emphasis upon diet, recognizing that diet was a major problem. Poor diet perhaps more than any other single factor threatens the child's ability to learn. If we are indeed what we eat, the child subsisting on a junk-loaded diet is a deprived child whose mental faculties may be impaired. Correct the diet and you modify the child's behavior; at that point, you have at least made a start toward alleviating your child's learning difficulties.

A doctor of my breadth of experience should be quite beyond shock. But I continue to be appalled by the dietary profiles of my young patients. Time and time again a youngster will tell me that by noon every day he has consumed four cans of some highly sweetened beverage or that he eats candy bars or Twinkies for breakfast. (Consider the examples being set for children:

former President Richard M. Nixon has confessed that during three years in the Oval Office his "breakfast" every day was a Milky Way.)

At the very beginning, I advise parents to remove certain foods altogether from their child's diet. At the top of the list are sugar and all foods and beverages containing sugar. This can be difficult, admittedly, if most of the calories he consumes are in some form of sugar. I also instruct them not to feed the child foods containing artificial colors, flavorings, and other additives. Beyond these restrictions, the child may have any number of food allergies; these can be discovered through conscientious elimination, or rotation, diets, or by allergy tests.

Which children show the most improvement and improve the most rapidly? There is no equation for measuring progress. In general, however, I can say that those children who are most cooperative about taking the prescribed substances and following the recommended diet are the ones likely to succeed fastest. Their success will be further implemented if they are blessed with understanding parents who recognize that we improve by steps and not by quantum leaps and that not all progress is always instantly visible.

Chapter IV

The New Approach

WHAT IS ORTHOMOLECULAR medicine? How does it work?

Orthomolecular medicine is the treatment of disease or disability by intensifying the concentrations of substances normally present in the human body and required for good health and optimum mental functioning. The quantity and the quality of our individual nutritional needs are dependent upon the metabolic profiles established genetically. Without the appropriate intake of substances sufficient to meet these needs, disorders of mind and body are likely to occur.

It was Linus Pauling, the Nobel Prize winner twice-honored for his contributions to chemistry and the cause of international peace, who in 1968 defined orthomolecular medicine as the achievement and the preservation of good health by provision of the optimum molecular environment for the mind. The prefix *ortho,* in addition to meaning "straight"—in the physical context—is sometimes used in the ethical sense to mean "correct" or "right." Orthomolecular, then, can simply be defined as "correct molecules." Synthetic drugs and other artificial substances have no place whatsoever in orthomolecular medicine.

The distinguished Huxley brothers, Sir Julian and Aldous, were forefathers of orthomolecular medicine. More than forty years ago, Sir Julian wrote, "Recent work has shown that vitamins and other accessory food factors have physical and mental effects far transcending what was originally thought possible." In the 1950s, brother Aldous observed that the nervous system is more vulnerable than the other tissues of the body: Consequently, vitamin deficiencies tend to affect the state of mind before they affect, at least in any very obvious way, the skin, the bones, mucus membranes, muscles, and viscera. The first result of an inadequate diet, he noted, is a lowering of the efficiency of the brain as an instrument for biological survival.

A century ago, a pioneer in brain chemistry, the Hessian nationalist Johann Ludwig Wilhelm Thudichum (1829–1901), who became England's first biochemist, accurately foretold some of the developments that were to occur in psychiatric research: "Many forms of insanity are unquestionably the external manifestations of the affects on the brain substance of poisons fermented within the body. These poisons we shall be able to isolate after we know the normal chemistry to its uttermost detail. Then will come the discoveries of the antidotes to the poisons and to the fermenting causes and processes that produce them."

These days, orthomolecular medicine is being administered successfully in many cases to improve the impaired body chemistry that results in such conditions as senility, alcoholism, degenerative diseases, hypoglycemia, and allergies, as well as learning disabilities and very severe mental disorders.

Treatment of learning disabilities and even severe mental illness, as well as bodily disease, is a matter, then, of increasing the concentration of substances—"right" molecules—usually present in the body. Instead of focusing on the minimum daily requirements of nutrients, orthomolecular medicine sets its sights on the *optimum* molecular environment that each and every one of the trillions of cells in the body needs for maximum mental and physical health.

When there are behavioral or physiological disorders, the chances are that the cells are not being adequately nourished. Cells have multiple needs. They need vitamins, amino acids, minerals, trace elements, essential fatty acids, phospholipids, prostaglandins, and many other substances necessary for optimal functioning. Fewer and fewer of these cellular "hungers" are being gratified by the foods we eat, as these foods become increasingly denutrified. So we must turn to supplementations to give our internal environment the nourishment it requires.

The functioning of the brain is dependent upon the composition and the structure—that is, upon the molecular environment—of the mind. The presence in the brain of the molecules of LSD, mescaline, or some other schizophrenogenic substance is associated with profound psychic effects. The phenomenon of general anesthesia also illustrates the dependence of the mind on its molecular constitution. If the mind is to function properly, the brain must have molecules of many different substances.

The brain consists of one quadrillion nerve-cell connections, or synapses, more than the total number of people who have lived since the brain evolved into its present form one hundred thousand years ago. These nerve cells can be linked to one another in more different ways than can the number of atoms presumed to exist in the entire universe.

A great deal of mental illness—and minimal brain dysfunction—results from a low concentration in the brain of any of the following vitamins: thiamine (B_1); nicotinic acid or nicotinamide (B_3); pyridoxine (B_6); biotin; ascorbic acid (C); and folic acid. There is evidence also that mental function and behavior are affected by changes in the configuration in the brain of glutamic acid, uric acid, and gamma-aminobutyric acid. A pathologically low level of vitamin B_{12} in the serum of the blood, to take just one example, occurs far more frequently in individuals afflicted with mental illness than it does in the general population. As we go along, we shall see how orthomolecular medicine applies other specific vitamins to the treatment of specific disabilities that occur so much more frequently among children than do severe disorders.

All psychological processes are dependent upon the harmonious equilibrium of chemicals both inside and outside the cells. A significant imbalance heralds trouble. Accepting this premise, we can say that the basis of orthomolecular medicine is the interaction of chemicals and the balance of chemicals in the body.

When I first began treating very sick patients, I discovered that inborn errors of metabolism render them vitally in need of an increased supply of vitamins far transcending the needs of the body for nourishment. Vitamins in measurements greater than the Recommended Daily Allowances enhance brain and body chemistry without inducing unpleasant side effects. What else could one conclude but that severe mental illnesses are of biochemical origin?

More and more, as time went on, my case file changed from very sick children to those greater numbers of children who are grouped under the umbrella term of "learning disabled." As my work with these boys and girls broadened, I became increasingly convinced that orthomolecular medicine could not be restricted to prescribed vitamins and minerals and amino acids. It must deal, and deal sternly, with dietary reform.

Day after day, in child after child, I was witnessing the results in the changes in eating habits that have evolved in the years after the Second World War. Even I was startled to learn the extent of the proliferating consumption of junk foods. My young patients (and too many of their parents) were subsisting on diets ridden with sugar, saturated fats, salt, and chemical additives. Modern food processing and packaging and aggressive advertising have taken their toll. It was impossible for me not to make the connection between these deteriorating eating habits and the increase in the incidence of learning, behavioral, and developmental problems among children. Diet had to be a causative factor in many of these difficulties.

There have been many studies to bring home the truth of this thesis. For example:

Forty-three of forty-five parents of hyperactive children (my patients) interviewed by Catherine Sayers Shwaery, of Alexandria, Virginia, reported that some foods, food colors, dyes, additives, or other ingredients in their children's diets caused them to be hyperactive, nervous, and irritable, and interfered with behavior and learning. The most frequently named antagonists, Mrs. Shwaery told me, were artificial colors (58 percent), sugar (53 percent), preservatives (33 percent), caffeine products (25 percent), artificial flavors (23 percent), and milk (23 percent). When the offending foods were removed from the diet and the children were given proper vitamin supplements, the overwhelming majority improved quickly and significantly.

We now know that even perfectly wholesome foods—among them, milk and wheat-derived products and certain fruits and vegetables containing a substance called salicylate—can be offending foods and produce hyperactive behavior, endangering academic careers and social maturation. It is necessary, therefore, to examine carefully the total diet of the child. We must not only proscribe the bad foods, we should not even take *good* foods for granted. We must eliminate anything and everything to which the child may be having sensitive reactions.

I have now treated thousands of learning disabled children with these enlightened procedures. The overwhelming majority of them improve remarkably. Even those who fail in all other forms of treatment respond to the natural, synergistic approach that combines high dosages of vitamins and minerals with a nutritionally superior diet.

You as parents should gear yourselves for your child's success in school. This suggests you will want to do everything in your power to make that success possible. First, you will need to equip your child to become capable of learning. Because learning disabilities are so often mistaken for something else, parents receive much cruel criticism. They are accused of being ineffective, of being negligent or poor disciplinarians, even of not caring. And when they do seek help for their child's erratic behavior, they may be regarded as aggressive, overanxious, or neurotic. After the diagnosis of learning disability is made, they fall unwarrantedly into a slough of guilt, and their guilt feelings are reinforced by officious friends and relatives, even by some professionals. They become vulnerable and fall prey to the frustration of receiving different and often contradictory advice from all kinds of "specialists" who cannot agree about these types of childhood problems.

You as parents may rightly feel, in short, that you are damned if you do and damned if you don't. But I believe you can take heart that we are moving into a time when there will be increasing knowledge about such complexities as the identification and the care of learning disabled children.

By accepting your shadow child and loving him without illusion or undue expectation, you can help him appreciate himself as he is, and inculcate within him his need for self-discipline. You can help him develop skills requisite for the world he lives in and deepen his awareness of the beautiful and the interesting things he can enjoy right now. You can help to arouse his curiosity and an interest in other people and teach him how to make and keep friends. You can enable him, even before his difficulties are resolved, to live as normal a life as possible and to feel secure about his own worth and the solid foundation of his family's support.

Chapter V

Preparing for the Orthomolecular Program

As I HAVE indicated, prior to a first visit I request that the prospective young patient have blood and hair tests and that his parents respond to a detailed questionnaire to the best of their ability.

The complete questionnaire begins on page 175. Here are a few of the questions taken at random.

Did the child rock in his crib as a baby?

During the child's first 2 years, did he like to be held?

Before age 3, did the child have an unusually good memory?

Does the child (age 3–5) show an *unusual* degree of skill (much better than normal child his age) at any of the following:
    Assembling jigsaw or similar puzzles
    Arithmetic computation
    Can tell day of week a certain date will fall on

Perfect musical pitch
Throwing and/or catching a ball

At what age did the child say his first words (even if
later stopped talking)?

The blood sampling gives us one set of facts. From the hair
analysis we gain a storehouse of information of quite another
sort.

Often, the blood sampling will reveal that the child has
borderline anemia or an iron deficiency. (Nearly 35 percent of
all babies are iron-deficient, making it the most prevalent nutritional disorder in the country.) If I detect a physical disability
of any kind, I will refer the child back to his pediatrician or
family doctor for a physical examination. (I do not serve as the
primary doctor.)

To give us a biochemical profile, the blood sampling is tested
to make twenty-five determinations, six for liver function and
kidney function. We also learn of thyroid function, cholesterol
and triglyceride levels, as well as evaluations of sodium, potassium, chloride, and carbon dioxide.

A blood sampling measures the degree of immediate exposure
there has been to such substances as lead, cadmium, arsenic,
and mercury. Many children with hyperkinetic behavior and/
or learning problems, we now know, have had too much prox-
imity to toxic metals and chemicals.

Blood measures nutrients, but only those still present at the
time of the test. We cannot conclude that the nutrients are
being transported through the cell membranes into the nucleus
of the cells where they are needed to provide nourishment. Nor
is a blood test particularly helpful in taking the cumulative
level of heavy metals. It can measure those that have just entered
the body, but cadmium in particular stays there only briefly,
so a test could reveal a level to be erroneously low.

The better the state of a child's nutrition, the less toxic metals will accumulate. Hair analysis, in contrast with blood sampling, gives the most accurate picture available of this accumulation. It also records trace element levels over the previous few months. These elements linger in the hair, as a matter of fact, at concentrations that are generally at least ten times higher than those present in blood serum and urine.

Every single hair grows out of a living cell. If a nutrient is lacking in that cell, it will be lacking as well in that single hair. Hair grows one-half to three-quarters of an inch per month, and the inch of hair closest to the scalp is an index to the mineral level in the cells for the current month.

In taking a hair sample, a measured amount of hair (approximately 0.4 grams) should be clipped from the nape of the neck and close to the scalp, the closer to the scalp the better. Five, six, or seven areas should be clipped. Thinning shears can be used.

At the laboratory, the hair sample is dissolved in acid. An absorption spectrometer analyzes it to determine the quantities of various nutrients and toxins. Hair can be analyzed quickly, and the report leaves the laboratory within twenty-four to forty-eight hours.

Concentration of trace elements in the hair provides a tool for the treatment of some conditions of illness. Recently, it has provided information about the diagnosis of hypoglycemia. Low levels or below normal levels of manganese and/or chromium correlate in most cases with a clinical diagnosis of hypoglycemia. At Children's Hospital Medical Center in Boston, it was found that children with cystic fibrosis have in their hair five times the normal amount of cadmium but only about 10 percent of the normal concentration of tightly bound calcium. Zinc deficiencies in the diet can be identified by below normal concentrations of zinc in the hair. Hair is also an index to high levels of lead and cadmium, which may produce the toxic effects leading to hyperactivity. Inasmuch as the major source of the entry of cadmium into the body is cigarette smoke, parents who smoke and siblings who smoke create a hazard by placing the child in the role of a passive smoker.

Hair is easily collected without frightening or hurting the child. How much gentler it is to snip off a few curls from the back of the head than to prick a vein to take blood. The analysis is as inexpensive as it is painless. The cost of a hair analysis for minerals is twenty-eight dollars; blood tests for nutrient and toxic minerals can range up to hundreds of dollars.

Hair analysis remains a controversial subject. It has its detractors who claim to find no merit in it. But as a diagnostic technique, it has for good reason been enjoying a renascence. I find that it can be predictive even of future health problems. In revealing levels of chromium, which has as its major function the establishment of proper glucose metabolism, it becomes especially desirable for use among children.

I foresee that hair analysis will become a routine part of multiphasic screening. There are hundreds of medical doctors who are already using it as a diagnostic tool (perhaps far more than admit they do). It does, after all, give a measurement of the levels of twenty-five or more different elements.

"Hair-tissue analysis has been instrumental in helping health-care professionals provide lifesaving diagnoses," as Dr. Garry F. Gordon, of Hayward, California, said in a letter in *The New York Times.* "As a diagnostic screening aid, it is used daily throughout the United States and abroad by reputable physicians. Hair analysis is the most cost-effective screening procedure available today to identify those in our population who are environmentally exposed to potentially toxic minerals. . . ."

I feel strongly that every hyperactive child should have a hair analysis to determine his lead, cadmium, and mercury levels; if a child's behavior suddenly undergoes great changes and he is constantly irritable and having temper tantrums, I usually suspect lead contamination. Lead is an irritant to the brain. I recall asking one boy, about whom I had my suspicions, if he chewed newspapers or magazines; lead is used in the printing process. He said he did not. I asked his mother about the family's housing. She told me that they lived on the ground floor of an apartment house. After a question or two more, I learned that the rooms faced an automobile service garage. Vehicles were in and out of there all the time. Engines were being tuned while the exhaust was spewing lead into the air, lead that found its way into the apartment. Car exhaust is the commonest source of lead in the human body. However, it has been proven by researchers in Great Britain that lead had been an environmental pollutant of our planet long before the internal combustion engine was invented. Samples of ice taken from the ages-old polar ice cap have revealed evidence of lead.

Lead poisoning was thought to be limited mostly to ghetto children. Most children of the streets not only inhaled lots of car exhaust but took lead into their system through the paint, dirt, and plaster they licked and breathed. Today, the prevalence of lead has been democratized. It is in the very air everyone breathes. Increasing amounts of it are found in the water we drink and the food we eat. The instances of mild to severe lead toxicities are on the rise; the potential damage to children is staggering.

Even small amounts of lead endanger children, yet I continue to find heavy concentrations in the tissues. Children are more vulnerable to lead pollution because their body weight is less and they therefore take in relatively greater quantities of lead from the environment. They inhale more air per unit of body weight because of their higher metabolic rates and greater physical activities. Lead levels in the blood high enough to produce poisoning can bring on mental retardation, depression, and seizures by altering the biochemistry of the brain. The children most prone to lead poisoning are those who eat lead-based paints.

Even more lethal than lead is the omnipresent toxic metallic element cadmium. The major source of cadmium is cigarette smoke. A high level of cadmium in the hair analysis of a child is telltale evidence of cigarette-smoking parents. High ratios of cadmium to zinc in the kidneys are associated with hypertension-related deaths. Selenium—a nonmetallic element of the sulfur family—is, like zinc, an antidote to dangerous accumulations of cadmium and mercury. Anemia caused by the ingestion of cadmium has been effectively treated with vitamin C. Slow-baked beans, slow-baked apples, and the sulfur amino acids cysteine and methionine can reduce the levels of toxic minerals. But the entire deposits cannot be completely removed, because they are environmental pollutants and are constantly entering our bodies.

To safeguard a child's brain, we must clean up the polluted environment from which toxic metals are absorbed into the body. The principal antagonists are lead, cadmium, mercury, and arsenic, which is used in pesticides sprayed on fruits and vegetables. If copper accumulates in the cells in large amounts, it behaves like a toxic mineral; it can be removed by zinc.

One takes encouragement where one finds it. I was heartened to read of a Midwestern college professor who acted on his conviction that lead "has the potential of undermining the mentality of our society." He goes so far as to ask visitors to remove their shoes at the door so they don't track in lead from the topsoil and the sidewalks. He has called for nothing less than a total ban on lead in gasoline and paint.

Trace minerals are essential nutrients, but in ninety-five out of one hundred children I find a lower than optimum level of three or more minerals. The most frequent deficiencies are of zinc, manganese, and chromium.

The trace mineral zinc must be in sufficient supply if the body is to benefit from its B_6 intake. I am convinced that what many people regard as a well-rounded diet does not provide sufficient amounts of either zinc or manganese. These two substances are important in combatting the excesses of toxic metals in the system.

Beyond the blood and hair examinations, I also suggest to the parents that their child have a physical examination if there hasn't been one recently. There may be undiscovered physiological sources of his difficulty. I urge the parents to be present during the examination, to ask questions and to demand answers.

"Dr. Cott, should he have a CAT scan?" a parent will sometimes ask me.

"One can easily be arranged, but I do not recommend it. My personal feeling is that they are being overprescribed. I do use CAT scans with my schizophrenic patients when I am not satisfied with the EEG report."

Nor do I usually suggest that a glucose tolerance test be administered. This test takes five hours and is especially stressful for young children, for blood is drawn seven times. I recommend this test only when I suspect from a family history of diabetes that the child may have a predisposition to diabetes. However, if a child is ten to twelve years old and has this familial background, or if hyperactivity is present and I find low levels of manganese and/or chromium in the hair analysis, I order the glucose tolerance test. These are the instructions I give:

1. Call the laboratory for an appointment, which is usually set for nine in the morning.

2. The child should have a diet rich in carbohydrates and sweet foods in the three to four days prior to the test. If niacin is being taken, substitute niacinamide in the week prior to the test.

3. Nothing to eat after seven o'clock on the night before the test, nor any beverages with calories. Water is permissible.

4. On the morning of the test, the child must not eat or drink anything, not even water, and must not chew gum. During the test, he must consume nothing but the sugar drink provided by the laboratory.

As for batteries of psychological investigation, here again I am somewhat negative. Perhaps I would be less skeptical if at the same time inquiry was being made into the diet or perceptual problems of the child. The cost of these tests is prohibitive for most families. A workup for the hyperactive child at a university clinic could well run to $2,500 or more. So much expensive testing and parental worry can be avoided if a parent is in the hands of a perceptive doctor and knows what questions to ask.

A hearing problem that has nothing to do with deafness may be the prime contributor to a learning disorder. A malfunctioning brain can affect hearing as much as a disorder in the ears. Strange or stumbling speech may be caused by a hearing disability, as may the failure to pay attention or to follow directions. The child physically *hears* as well as the next person, but somehow what is being heard is not translating into a message because he suffers from a lack of auditory discrimination. It serves no use to have this child tested for sounds per se; that is, how faint a tone he can hear. An appointment with an audiologist, however, will yield a complete evaluation, which includes the testing of impedance; impedance gauges how the brain perceives what the ears hear.

The examination of a child who suffers from a disorder of speech, communication, or learning cannot be considered complete without a visual examination. The investigation of sight and vision is as important as any other part of the total examination—and *more* important and revealing than many other routines.

Most of the children I have treated have had examinations that included electroencephalograms. But very few have been examined for vision by a vision specialist. If an examination had been done, it was performed for sight. If in that instance the child demonstrated 20/20 vision on the Snellen chart, the parents were told there was nothing wrong with their child's eyes. This may be true for distance eyesight, but it overlooks all the near-point visual activity so crucial to the dynamic visual process of reading.

The child who has a school or a learning problem must have an examination performed by a specialist who investigates the function of the eyes as well as their structure. Such a specialist could be an ophthalmologist (an M.D. specializing in diseases of the eye) or an optometrist, who specializes in developmental vision. At the present time, few ophthalmologists perform these examinations, so one is more apt to find a developmental vision specialist among optometrists.

Let me make this important distinction: Sight is the ability of the eye to see clearly; it refers only to the capacity for resolving detail. Vision is the ability to gain meaning from what is seen.

Too often, parents are lulled into a false sense of security when they are told their child's eyes are "fine," when indeed they may not be. There can be significant deviations from normal vision on that 20/20 Snellen chart reading. Farsightedness can be overlooked in a distance-vision screening examination, for example, and thus cause difficulties when a child tries to do close-up work.

There can be problems if one eye is different from the other in refractive power. Convergence of the eyes noseward for looking at things close-up is also of vital importance in centering with two eyes on a near-point task. Convergence bears an important relationship to focusing; the two processes are combined. If this link is not proper, a child can be out of focus and be completely unaware that he is, just as a child who sees a separate image with each eye has no way of telling us about this because he believes everybody else sees in the same way. The out-of-focus child cannot tell us about his blurred vision until he can be helped to see in sharp focus with the aid of lenses.

So many of the children I have treated have not been able to see near things in sharp focus or to look at the world through binocular vision until their eyes were treated successfully by a developmental optometrist or by an ophthalmologist specializing in developmental vision. Yet these children are trying every day to learn to read a printed page that presents nothing but a blur. Lack of smooth muscle control in the eye makes it a difficult task to follow successive words in a line of print as the eyes sweep across a page. Often the eyes will not make the repeated necessary convergences if the focusing is not proper; thus, the child will skip words in the line, lose his place, or be unable to find the word on the next line. As a result, he will not comprehend what he reads. Significantly, hyperactivity is frequently reduced when the visual systems work efficiently.

Locomotion is generally considered to be the first step in

the development of vision. A baby begins to move not only his eyes but also his whole body, and thus he starts to locate objects in the environment and become familiar with them. Labels are given to these objects by family members and learned by the baby. Language develops around the use of these labels, so out of this process known as vision, physical sight will coalesce with understanding and intelligence under normal circumstances. But any malfunction in this system can cause defects in functional vision.

Developmental visual training is another vital link in the creation of an optimum molecular environment for the mind. Neither improved nutrition, vitamin and mineral supplements, enriched educational opportunities, nor visual and perceptual motor training alone can be successful in fully helping the child who has learning disabilities. *All* must be used in a coordinated program to develop each child's potential.

Now your child is ready. The tests I wish all my prospective young patients to take have been done, and any other tests that may be indicated in his particular case have been completed. And you have answered the questionnaire.

You are ready to take your child for consultation with an orthomolecular doctor.

In the next chapter, I shall show you how the orthomolecular therapy begins and what you must do to carry out the program successfully.

Chapter VI

Administering the Orthomolecular Program

YOU HAVE ARRIVED for a consultation involving your learning disabled child. I have before me the results of your child's blood and hair tests and the questionnaire you completed. It is the time to review the findings with you before the program for treatment begins. It is also the time for me to recommend a glucose tolerance test if one is indicated and to suggest a vision or a hearing test if the profile revealed by the questionnaire suggests there may be problems with these senses.

Frequently, the hair analysis will reveal that your child's lead level is elevated. If that is indeed the case, I administer a natural chelating agent. Chelation (the word is derived from the Greek *chela*, meaning "claw") is the process by which the medication combines with the lead—or with any other heavy metal present in the tissues—to form a new compound that is soluble and can be discharged by the body. I usually administer a high-sulfur amino acid supplement such as methionine or cysteine and suggest that slow-baked beans and/or slow-baked apples be eaten several times a week. Toxic metals cannot be completely removed from the system; they are pervasive in the environment, as we all know, and they are entering our bodies every day, no matter where we live. But their levels can be diminished drastically by administering vitamins C and E and either of the high-sulfur amino acids. Selenium is used to lower the level of mercury, and zinc can reduce high levels of copper.

"Encouraging results with the orthomolecular approach can be quick and dramatic," I explain. "But more commonly, it can take two to six months before any significant improvement becomes apparent. Considering what you have been through, I hope you can be patient long enough to give the treatment a proper trial. Your child will improve in his own good time, but only if the program is followed strictly."

At the same time, I warn against being deceived by any positive change that may occur quite early. This is no signal to stop treatment. But orthomolecular medicine is by no means a never-ending treatment, as psychoanalysis has become for some people. The question "How long will it take, Dr. Cott?" is routinely asked by parents, and I respond that in general they should expect to have the treatment continue for at least two to three years. But in most cases where compliance is good, sufficient results should be seen within a three-month period to encourage continuing the program. I always hope that the changes in the child's diet will become permanent, but after the two- or three-year period we can begin to reduce and phase out the regimen of prescribed substances.

Even at this point there are parental fears I must assuage. There may still be some lingering suspicion that the child is retarded just because his academic performance does not equal that of his peers. The parents probably have been told as much by teachers and other professionals, but once again I reassure them that this is not an accurate assessment. Their child is learning disabled, not retarded or stupid or lazy.

I try to communicate with the child at whatever level may be comprehensible to him. If he is of school age, I am eager to have him understand that because he is not able to learn as easily and as quickly as his classmates at the moment, it does not mean that he is any less bright or capable. I tell him that we will be starting a program that can help him to make the best use of his abilities and catch up with the others. It will mean giving up some of the things he likes to eat and drink, but in their place will be foods and beverages that will make him feel so much better and that he will grow to like very much. I also tell him I will be prescribing some very good substances that are *not* medicine but are like food.

"We all have new experiences as we go through life," I say to the child. "Life is full of changes. If we don't keep in step with them, we fall behind. We all discover as we go along that we would be better off if we started doing some things differently. In your case, by taking your tablets and capsules and eating good foods you will be feeling better and everything will go more easily for you. It will be a much nicer life for you."

If the child is especially hyperkinetic, I make no effort to bridle his destructive, distracting behavior. My interest is in causes. When we get to the root of the problem, the symptoms will begin to disappear of their own accord. Why reprimand or try to harness a child who can't help the way he is mis-behaving? Why chastise a child who would like to behave differently but cannot . . . or who would welcome rest but cannot rest because he is driven by an internal force beyond his control?

I make it my business to reassure the parents about the sub-stances I will be prescribing for their child. I emphasize that there are no serious side effects, if any at all, regardless of what they might have read or heard in the sensationalizing media. It seems so elementary, but I must repeat and repeat: Vitamins

49

and minerals are food substances, not drugs or medications. (As I write this, there is a furor over the alleged deaths of thirty-eight premature infants who were given a vitamin E solution. It was *not* the vitamin E itself that was injurious, of course, but the solution in which it was dissolved.)

On my orthomolecular advisory, I indicate those substances—sugar- and starch-free; no artificial colors or flavors— I wish the child to have and the amount and the frequency of intake. Parents are counseled to supervise this daily regimen faithfully. Below is the list of substances I work with. From them I prescribe, in appropriate dosages, to fit each child's particular needs.

Niacinamide (vitamin B_3)

Niacin (vitamin B_3)

Ascorbic acid (vitamin C)

Pyridoxine (vitamin B_6)

Thiamine (vitamin B_1)

Cyanocobalamin (vitamin B_{12})

Riboflavin (vitamin B_2)

Vitamin A

Vitamin E

Vitamin C

Vitamin B-complex

Phenylalanine

Methionine

Cysteine

Tryosine

Tryptophan

Oil of Evening Primrose

Chelated calcium

Chelated magnesium

Manganese

Zinc gluconate

Chelated zinc

Multivitamin-minerals
  (copper-free)

Lecithin (triple-strength)

Selenium

G.T.F. Chromium

PABA

Pangamic acid (vitamin B$_{15}$)   Folic acid

Biotin   Multi-Jet powder

Calcium pantothenate   L-glutamine

None of the substances I recommend is a drug or a medication. All are non-prescription and are freely sold over the counter. They can be bought at almost any pharmacy or even in some supermarkets, and you will need nothing signed by a doctor to procure them. A vitamin-mineral supplement is really a food item, not a pharmacological compound.

Previously, on the phone or through correspondence, I will have cautioned parents that as simple as it may sound the orthomolecular treatment is not totally a self-help program requiring no professional guidance. The diagnosis of learning disabled may be accurate enough, but there is a great deal more we must know about the child before we start giving him elevated amounts of vitamins and minerals. I make clear, too, that the supplements are only part of the program and that failure to improve the nutritional status of the child can result in only minimal gains. Once the child does begin treatment, the parents must assume the responsibility for administering the regimen, with whatever direction is needed from the doctor.

Sometimes on my lecture tours a perplexed parent will put to me, "But if there's no orthomolecular doctor in this area, what am I to do? As you explain the treatment, Dr. Cott, it sounds simple enough for someone to undertake on his own."

I cannot give parents any "do-it-yourself" encouragement for initiating treatment on their own. The child must have tests and a personal consultation before a program can be tailored to his specific needs. There are hundreds of doctors who are now committed to the orthomolecular approach. Surely it can't be too much of a sacrifice, when the stakes are so high, to find one who will supervise the child's entry into this type of intervention. Most of us are psychiatrists. Many of us were using traditional therapies to treat mildly or severely disordered children before becoming convinced that a biochemical approach—combining prescribed nutrient substances with improved dietary habits—was the superior, more expeditious way to address these disabilities successfully. There are practitioners of orthomolecular medicine in most of the large cities and in virtually every state in the United States, and in Canada. Please write or phone me if you need help in finding an orthomolecular physician: Allan Cott, M.D., 160 East 38th Street, New York, New York (212-679-5593 or 212-679-6694).

We have found that a child, pound for pound, can accommodate himself to dosages of vitamins even more easily than an adult. We don't know why this is. I can only speculate that it is because they are growing and their regular requirements for vitamins may be greater than is generally assumed and they have no negative notions about supplementations.

Nevertheless, I adhere to caution in introducing orthomolecular treatment to very young children. If the child weighs less than 35 pounds, I prescribe a daily dosage of 100 mg. of niacinamide (vitamin B_3) and 100 mg. of vitamin C, and I gradually increase the amounts I give to larger and older children. Depending on the severity of the child's disorder, significantly higher amounts of certain substances may be prescribed. Only the doctor can be the judge of how much is indicated.

With children weighing between 35 and 45 pounds, I begin the treatment with daily dosages of the following basic substances and amounts:

niacinamide (vitamin B_3): 100–200 mg.
pyridoxine (vitamin B_6): 100–400 mg.

riboflavin (vitamin B$_2$): 100–200 mg.
ascorbic acid (vitamin C): 250–500 mg.
calcium pantothenate: 100–400 mg.
vitamin B-complex: 1 tablet daily
magnesium: 75–200 mg.
zinc: 10–30 mg.

If a child weighs more than 45 pounds, I try to reach quite rapidly the optimum daily maintenance level of about 1–2 grams of niacinamide, equal amounts of ascorbic acid, and 200–400 mg. of pyridoxine and riboflavin.

I do not want to start the child with dosages so high that they might cause some unpleasantness and build up resistance for going on with treatment. Any side effects that do occur, I repeat, are rare, superficial—and transient. Occasionally, niacinamide will cause nausea. Ascorbic acid sometimes brings on diarrhea or frequent urination. These reactions indicate some degree of intolerance and invariably subside when I reduce the dosage.

Let me say once more, I have *never* seen a serious side effect from the megadoses used in orthomolecular treatment. Any reported instances of adverse effects of megadoses can be assumed to have occurred without the proper supervision. So let me emphasize that all substances ingested should be administered responsibly and with a clear understanding of what could constitute an "overdose."

I frequently supplement the basic four substances of niacinamide, pyridoxine, ascorbic acid, and calcium pantothenate with thiamine (vitamin B$_1$), riboflavin (vitamin B$_2$), vitamin E, folic acid, and certain amino acids, and I prescribe these in varying amounts to meet the needs of the child. But niacinamide (vitamin B$_3$), ascorbic acid (vitamin C), and pyridoxine (vitamin B$_6$) are the most important components in the treatment program. The mineral prescription is based on the deficiencies found in the analysis done on the hair. These vitamins (along with vitamin E) facilitate the respiration of all tissues; satisfactory tissue respiration is necessary if the brain is to function properly.

"These supplements are available as tablets, capsules, liquids, and as a soluble powder," I explain to the parent. "Nearly all vitamin tablets produced by drug manufacturers are coated with artificial colors ranging from pale pastel shades to dark blues and deep reds. These colors are made from synthetic dyes. The tablets also have fillers comprised of sugar or cornstarch and a variety of chemical additives. For these reasons, I hope you will not stock up with such tablets. Because of their contents, they can offset the therapeutic value of the supplements. The artificial colors can increase a hyperactive child's behavior problems."

I find it regrettable that if manufacturers must add color to tablets to make them "attractive," or psychologically palatable, they do not use pigments that are demonstratively additive-free. If orange is an enticing color, why not use the orange from the carotene of carrots? Or why not green from chlorophyll? Or red from beets? (The only naturally colored vitamins are riboflavin, which is a yellowish-orange, and B_{12}, which is red.)

I also dissuade parents from buying liquid vitamins. This form of supplement contains preservatives, mold retardants, and glycerine; the latter ingredient is used to prevent possible freezing during shipment. In addition, liquid vitamins have artificial colorings, flavorings, and sweeteners.

I recommend the capsule or tablet form. But for children who cannot swallow pills, the soluble powder can be used. It contains a mixture of all vitamins and most minerals.

As I have said, certain amino acids—most commonly methionine, cysteine, and tryptophan, and to a lesser extent L-glu-

22222

tamine—become part of my treatment as warranted. There are twenty-odd amino acids of which eight are known as essential. They are essential because they cannot be manufactured in the body and must be provided by the food we eat. These eight essential amino acids are leucine, isoleucine, lysine, methionine, phenylalanine, tryptophan, threonine, and valine.

I use two amino acids and several vitamins and minerals, as I have mentioned, as chelating agents for reducing levels of toxic metals such as lead, cadmium, and mercury. For the child who is having difficulty sleeping through the night—a common symptom of the learning disabled—I add tryptophan to the treatment. Tryptophan is both a sedative and an antidepressant. Niacinamide (vitamin B_3) given at bedtime is extremely valuable for sleep because it increases the REM (rapid eye movement) stage of sleep by 40 percent. Inositol, one of the ingredients of lecithin, is also effective for good, restful sleep. Two other amino acids—phenylalanine and tyrosine—also have value as antidepressants, because they are precursors of brain transmitters.

In general, the amino acids are vital in the building of strong tissues, and they play an important role in the treatment of various diseases. Their practical application in medical and pharmaceutical fields is wide. Again, depending on the age and the weight of the child, I administer dosages of the various amino acids ranging from 200 mg. daily to 500 mg. twice daily.

Even at this juncture, when a parent has made a commitment to the orthomolecular approach, she will ask, "If penicillin cures pneumonia, why can't Ritalin cure hyperactivity?"

"Hyperactivity is not a simple, specific condition resulting from one specific cause," I respond. (She may have asked me the same question two or three times previously.) "There can be so many causes: brain injury due to trauma before, during, or after birth; the mother's health and general nutrition before conception and during pregnancy; lack of nutrients; sensitivity to certain chemicals in the environment; sensory deprivation; heredity; emotional factors; or stress."

It is worth taking the time and the effort to ease her mind on this question once and for all. Ritalin will tranquilize her child, as she has probably observed, and increase his attention span. But Ritalin does not come to grips with allergies or hypoglycemia or other biochemical imbalances, which, if untreated, will still remain and perhaps worsen. Increasingly, large dosages of this drug might become necessary to keep a child's behavior under control. But it will not equip him to cope with his underlying problems at school, at home, and in the world at large.

Inveigh as I do so strenuously against the routine practice of prescribing drugs, I myself, as I have stated, do *selectively* recommend Ritalin or some other "tranquilizing" medication. But this is only a temporary measure, at the start of treatment, and the prescription serves the pragmatic goal of keeping the child in school and making him more bearable at home. I assure the parents that at the earliest possible time I want their child completely off any medication. That time occurs when we see the beginning of progress under the natural, non-noxious orthomolecular regimen of wholesome foods and nutrient supplements.

"This sounds all well and fine," a mother will grant. "In theory. But what does this do for dyslexia? Are all the vitamins in the world going to make my child know the difference between *d-o-g* and *g-o-d*?"

I reply, "I have never claimed that orthomolecular treatment is the total solution for a child's learning problems. What I do claim is that by sorting out the crossed circuits in the brain of a child, that child becomes infinitely more capable of learning. Then he will require the remedial coaching that will help him grow out of his specific reading disability."

Of greatest importance to most dyslexic children is the removal by chelating agents of lead, cadmium, and mercury from the body. Any reduction in these toxic metals produces noticeable clinical results: a *decrease* in hyperactivity and an *increase* in serenity. In so many dyslexic children, as in children with other learning problems, I find a definite correlation between high levels of lead and cadmium and low or below normal levels of calcium and magnesium. We know how to correct this undesirable profile.

"Please keep in touch," I ask the parents at that first consultation. "Within two weeks I want to hear either on the telephone or through the mail how things are going. You can always call me or make an appointment to see me if you think it is necessary. In any event, I would like to see you and your child again in a month."

Subsequently, I do not need to see the child more than every other month or so. But I do encourage the parents to write from time to time so that I can monitor progress. If there should be any negative reaction to the nutrient supplements, I can tell the parent which one is most likely to be producing the effect, how much to reduce the dose, and when and how to build up again to the optimal regimen.

The orthomolecular approach, then, has a number of advantages to commend it to most learning disabled children. The parent, in essence, becomes "the doctor." The sustained and considerable expense of confrontational therapy involving long-term psychological counseling and the endless filling of prescriptions is avoided. Vitamins and minerals cost the smallest fraction of any psychotropic drug prescribed for disordered children. There is no complex machinery or technology. This child becomes a more "economical child" also, because the improvement in his diet alone eliminates so many trips to the doctor that can be traced to malnutrition or undernutrition.

Orthomolecular medicine can be applied as a preventive as well as a therapeutic measure. It could easily be included in prenatal care. It would be perfectly safe—and beneficial—for pregnant women to insure their supreme nutrition by taking elevated dosages of vitamins and minerals under their doctor's supervision.

Orthomolecular treatment will strengthen a child's defenses against the harmful factors increasingly present in the environment. Resistance will further be strengthened if the child is receiving excellent nutrition through the foods he eats. As well as "straightening out" learning impairments, the combination of the orthomolecular substances and wholesome food can only enhance general health and promote physical growth. Does this mean that *all* children could profit from taking vitamins and minerals in the amounts recommended for the learning disabled child? I think not. In the orthomolecular approach, we are basically correcting an imbalance of brain chemistry that does not exist among other children. Supplements, yes, to compensate for what is lacking in most diets; megadosages, no.

There is seriously uninformed criticism of the orthomolecular treatment. The water-soluble vitamins and minerals, it is asserted, are not stored in the body; therefore, the high dosages taken are essentially wasted because they are rapidly excreted. I respond with this simple but irrefutable fact: The learning disabled child (or the severely disordered child) requires for the realignment of his brain chemistry substances many, many times that of the Recommended Daily Allowances. These substances perform a role quite different from their commonplace use as a dietary supplement. Megadosages of vitamins and minerals act more like a benign drug, and they do effect that change in brain chemistry that enables a child to become teachable. They enter biochemical pathways and alter levels of neurotransmitters. Neurotransmitters are formed in the brain and carry electrical impulses from one brain cell to the next in a complex web involving a quadrillion cells.

Critics become inadvertently amusing when they suggest that discernible benefits from the orthomolecular approach are purely psychological. They also go astray when they predict that a change of diet for a disturbed child would lead to family friction; too much attention gets focused on that child, they say, and others in the family feel coerced if they must follow his dietary restrictions. Other critics of the same persuasion claim that the interest and the attention invested in the child are responsible for the improvement. Many parents have reported dismay and disbelief when their family doctor dismisses their question on the value of nutrients with the sarcastic advice, "If you want your child to have expensive urine, give him vitamins." (More than one mother has said to me, in effect, "It almost seems as if the whole family were in treatment. We are pretty much sticking to my son's diet, and I think we are all feeling better and more energetic because of the improved nutrition.") Our detractors also magnify the time, the effort, and the expense involved in a healthful, natural diet. The truth is that it is actually less expensive to eat wisely than poorly, and the time and the effort to put together simple but good meals can be inconsequential.

Again, I appeal to you, the parents. You are the prime movers in this drama of rescuing your learning disabled child from his torments. I urge you to take an informed attitude toward mental or emotional disorders. I plead with you to stop all wishful thinking—this, too, will *not* pass—and to recognize your child needs help. Your child is redeemable, his difficulties are treatable, and the sooner he receives help, the fewer will be his miseries and the more rapid will be his recovery.

Just the fact that you are reading this book suggests your receptiveness to innovation. You may be just one of the increasing thousands of parents who will choose orthomolecular therapy as the first and primary intervention, rather than come to it in frustration after other forms of treatment have been tried and found wanting.

In the following pages I encapsulate a few "case histories." They are representative of the experiences of learning disabled children who have been successfully reoriented through the orthomolecular approach.

Chapter VII

From My Case Files

Justin R.

THIS HYPERACTIVE, VERY difficult child began treatment when he was nine. He was depressed and suicidal. He was highly destructive in school and terrorized his teacher. His mother said Justin had lots of nausea and vomiting, and dizzy spells, and was always complaining about his aches and pains. He "saw" things. He was a slow learner, but he could do extraordinary things around the house that required electrical acumen.

Family history was not in his favor. There was alcoholism, obesity, and diabetes. Justin drank a quart of milk and a quart of a sugary orange drink every day and ate half a loaf of bread at a sitting and tablespoons of sugar right out of the bowl.

He was having difficulties in all subjects and was performing below grade level. He was given a prescription of supplements and taken off bread, milk, sugar, and orange drink for several weeks. His learning disability came from perceptual problems due to his having been "drunk" most of the time on the milk, the orange drink, and the bread. Within one year after the

61

change in diet and the introduction of megavitamin therapy, he was functioning normally in a regular classroom. He received an award for being the most improved student in the school.

Justin had the good fortune of having parents who were extremely cooperative. Most of all, he became his own best friend, with a heightened interest in getting better. When he ate something that made him sick, he would take a dose of salts and make a firm resolve never to eat that food again.

Johnny D.

This eight-year-old did no work at school, arrived late and left early, and was disruptive while he was in the classroom. He engaged in bizarre behavior, such as smearing blood all over his face from a small cut on his hand. His actions were impulsive and completely unpredictable. He was learning nothing, and his teacher concluded that something was so seriously wrong with him that he could not be dealt with at school. He seemed to be of normal intelligence, but his IQ score was around 80.

His mother told me that he had been hyperactive most of his life, but during the last two years he had been much worse. He was referred for help and was reported to be normal; he would grow out of his problem. But he did not, of course, and he continued to be very difficult at school and at home.

It may seem strange that any professional would consider a boy normal who thought that people were "watching" him, who saw faces in the air, who heard his name being called when it wasn't, who thought he could hear his own thinking inside his head, and who was sure that people were making fun of him and gossiping about him. He was extremely restless, irritable, and cranky. Johnny's treatment was started with two grams of niacinamide and one-half gram of pyridoxine to reduce his hyperactive behavior and to improve his disposition.

Johnny's recovery was so rapid as to be remarkable. Within two months he was calmer, feeling much better, getting good grades in school, and having less trouble getting along with his classmates. He received an excellent report from his astonished teacher, who had been quite hopeless about his prospects.

Joseph N.

At his first consultation, Joseph, though only eight years old, announced that he was hyperactive, hypoglycemic, and hyperopic (a visual defect more generally called farsightedness). Aside from these problems, he assured me that all was well. There was no doubt that he was a child of normal to superior intelligence. The perceptual handicap was obvious, and his behavior strongly suggested that he had many unresolved emotional difficulties.

I indeed discovered hypoglycemia, which interfered with his perceptions, associations, and thought processes in general. I also found high lead and cadmium levels. The boy did not sleep well at night.

My diagnosis was that he was a learning disabled child with minimal brain dysfunction. For his glucose intolerance, I prescribed a diet rich in protein, low in carbohydrate, and excluding all foods and beverages prepared with cane sugar, all foods containing artificial colors or flavors, and caffeinated beverages. Megavitamins were prescribed to reduce the lead and the cadmium levels.

Joseph improved gratifyingly. He was seventeen years old when I last saw him, a senior in a regular high school, holding down a job after school, on weekends, and during holidays, and was doing extremely well in all areas of his life.

David F.

Prior to coming to me when he was six years old, David had been put on Ritalin to modify his hyperactive behavior. But he suffered a marked weight loss, and when his mother took him off Ritalin his unruly conduct resumed.

David's background made his minimal brain dysfunction comprehensible, if not inevitable. His mother had been fatigued throughout pregnancy and was later diagnosed as suffering from hypoglycemia. David was born prematurely, and for the first three months of his life he had colic and diarrhea and continual spells of projectile vomiting. There was never a time in his life when his behavior could be said to be normal. He rocked a great deal in his crib. He never walked but was off on a run as soon as he could get on his own two feet. Between the ages of two and four, he bumped into people as though he did not see them. He was withdrawn and frequently whirled himself like a top, and he indulged in ritualistic behavior, even showing some signs of autism. His speech was not progressing; between the ages of three and five, he frequently repeated sentences and phrases he had just heard and used them in answering questions.

Aside from prescribing the orthomolecular vitamins and minerals, I put David on a restricted diet that eliminated wheat products as well as anything containing sugar, artificial flavors and colors, and other additives.

Quite quickly, David's attention span improved. But his mother was running into interference from his pediatrician, and I found myself writing to her, "The problems you are having with your pediatrician are well known to me, because very few pediatricians are open-minded enough to encourage a mother to try a treatment approach that has helped thousands upon thousands of children throughout the United States and elsewhere. These doctors do not hesitate for one moment to prescribe with impunity large doses of Ritalin; in the next breath, they are cautioning mothers against the use of large dosages of vitamins as being 'harmful' for the child."

David had a visual problem, and this presented more trouble; subsequently, I was writing his mother again: "It is unfortunate that most ophthalmologists do not address themselves to the visual functions. It is true that they know all there is to be known about organic disease of the eye, but because they do not believe that visual function is involved in learning disabilities, or in any other functional disorders, it is my observation that developmental optometrists are more reliable as specialists for the treatment of these conditions."

David had other sensitivities that had to be isolated. One of them was salicylates. He had to be deprived of apples and other foods, most of which were his favorites. We also discovered a milk sensitivity. Poor lad, he also was found to be allergic to feathers, mold, grasses, cats, dogs, dust, and pollen. I advised against any sedating medication for his occasional flare-ups, because they always had the adverse effect of making him even more hyperactive.

David has learned to live with both the treatment and all the restrictions that his susceptibilities place upon him. As a fourteen-year-old, he is coming along well and is keeping up with his classmates.

Sally V.

She first visited me when she was eleven years old. The diagnosis was minimal brain dysfunction and hyperinsulinism.

65

In the first weeks of her life, she was malnourished and did not gain weight properly. Diarrhea was an integral part of her history. She became a voracious eater and would put anything into her mouth, including bad-tasting medicines and sand and other nonedible substances. She stuffed her nose with bread and crayons. She was hyperactive, constantly moving, changing swiftly from one thing to another, and she went through a lot of finger manuevers and sometimes postured with her hands in bizarre positions. She wet the bed until she was nine years old. She had difficulty settling down in school. Her knees and ankles hurt her so much when she ran that she couldn't get to sleep at night. She had a schizophrenic uncle and a sister who was a depressive.

Complex as her difficulties sound, the road to improvement was quite simple. The megavitamin and mineral dosages and the removal of all sugar and additives from her diet proved sufficient. Her extraordinary mannerisms disappeared. Her appetite came under control. She no longer stuffed her mouth and her nose with alien substances. She was able to learn and had the improved report card as proof of it.

Miriam B.

As an infant, she disliked bright lights, bright colors, and unusual sounds. She was notably stiff and awkward to hold. She didn't like to wear new clothes. She seemed a bit dull. She would "look through" and "walk through" her parents. She was indifferent to being liked and was happiest when left alone. She was aloof, indifferent, self-contained, remote. She didn't respond well to questions. At one time, she was thought by her parents to be deaf. She exhibited some autistic-like behavior.

Miriam was seven years old when she was brought in for

From My Case Files

consultation. She was learning disabled and diagnosed as having minimal brain dysfunction. Her father had also been learning disabled. When Miriam was two and a half years old, her mother noticed that she would have a hyperkinetic reaction to a particular red-colored fruit juice. I suggested that it would be a good idea if Miriam were taken off all foods and beverages containing artificial flavors or colors. She took her vitamin prescription mashed up and mixed with honey. Within a month after beginning the program, she became peaceful. She could sit quietly. She concentrated better. Her mother was astonished with Miriam's sudden ability to organize her schoolwork.

Six months after treatment began, Miriam was reading at her own third-grade level. She was above average in math. She had become sociable, relating well with her peers. Her handwriting improved. After another six months, Miriam's mother wrote to tell me that Miriam's coordination continued to improve and she no longer had sleeping problems. Miriam was continuing to gain weight. I advised Mrs. B. that it was a good idea to keep on with the regimen of supplements that had been serving Miriam so well: vitamin C; methionine; vitamin B_6; calcium gluconate; magnesium gluconate; niacinamide; and a multivitamin tablet.

Marvin R.

Marvin, the oldest of eight children, was nine years of age when his father brought him in for consultation. Mr. R. reported that Marvin was learning well but that he was hyperactive and often a behavior problem in school. With some questioning, I discovered that Marvin's writing and reading were, in fact, below grade level and that he understood English but could not speak it. He had some speaking knowledge of Yiddish. To the basic orthomolecular substances, I added L-glutamine, silica, a multivitamin-mineral tablet, chewable lecithin tablets, and chelated chromium. Marvin began to improve steadily. His hyperactivity decreased and he no longer presented behavioral problems in school.

Marvin is a teenager now; he does well academically and has learned to apply himself.

Arnold J.

Arnold, eight years old when I first saw him, was hyperkinetic. He rocked back and forth. Because he was everywhere and into everything, he couldn't be taken to church, restaurants, or even other people's homes. Incredibly, Arnold's pediatrician said Arnold was not hyperactive.

Arnold ate like an adult and weighed almost one hundred pounds. Chocolate in particular set off his hyperactivity. I forbade all sweets. I put him on several supplementary substances beyond the standard, or basic, vitamin and mineral mix. His behavior at school and at home began to improve. Then there was a regression. Again, he could not sit still, and he was generally disruptive in the classroom. He sucked his left thumb for long periods. I suggested that he may have been eating sweets again. This was just after Easter, and his parents agreed that his fond grandparents may have given him a chocolate Easter bunny without their knowledge. After six months of treatment, Arnold was having few problems in school. His printing on paper had become "just beautiful" and his grades were vastly improved. But he had fallen into the practice of interrupting his teachers by talking out in the classroom whenever he had a question. He also felt superior to the other children, often calling them stupid when they gave a wrong answer to a question. A year after I first saw him, he had become successful in making friends and was taking delight in his classes. He was reading well, he particularly liked mathematics, and he was getting As and Bs on his report card.

Lois T.

This illegitimate six-year-old girl was brought to me by her aunt, who explained, "I wanted you to see her not so much because of any abnormal behavior but because for the past five years she has never been in a stable environment nor ever had a proper diet. She is prone to colds, and I would like a proper evaluation of her."

It turned out that Lois was hyperactive, constantly moving, changing quickly from one thing to another; and she lived in dread of animals, noises, fires, and burglars. She had just come into the custody of her aunt. Her early life had been chaotic. Both parents constantly abused alcohol and drugs and frequently argued and became physically violent with each other. It is likely that Lois's mother used drugs and alcohol all during the pregnancy, though the child was born normal and did not experience withdrawal symptoms. Given the addiction and the life-style of her parents, she was a child of neglect.

Because Lois could not swallow pills or capsules, her treatment was started with Multi-Jet powder (a soluble mixture of all vitamins and most minerals) and brewer's yeast tablets to supply chromium and selenium, which are not included in the Multi-Jet powder. She was also put on an orthomolecular regimen. For a time she continued to be destructive in the classroom, but academically she was doing well. She made many friends and developed a penchant for making other children laugh. She became a little charmer.

Presently, Lois overcame her irrational fears and quieted down. She was fortunate in having a concerned aunt who could anticipate trouble ahead before Lois became an advanced "case."

Chapter VIII

Treating Very Sick Children

I BEGAN MY PRACTICE of orthomolecular medicine with children, as I said earlier, by treating those who were seriously disabled. These children were classifiable as suffering from schizophrenia, autism, and Down's syndrome. Let us be grateful that the majority of learning disabled children have minimal brain dysfunction rather than the more severe developmental disorders.

The children who were first brought to me had been exposed to every form of treatment and to every known tranquilizer and sedative with little or no success even in controlling the hyperactivity.

Before the megavitamin approach was introduced, these very sick children were treated almost exclusively with psychotropic medications, but the practice of keeping them drugged had the paradoxical effect of increasing their intense hyperactivity, and occasionally there were other side effects. Typically, this pharmacological approach was in tandem with classical "talking" therapy. If there was one opinion I had come to hold strongly, it was that talking is unproductive when the patient is too troubled to participate rationally—or to participate at all.

From the start, I set as my goal *recovery,* not a becalmed, manageable patient. I made it my first priority to correct the brain chemistry of these children. Only then could psychological counseling become meaningful as an adjunct to the orthomolecular treatment. Parents who brought their children to me were relieved to realize that the injury to the child was nutritional and biochemical in origin and *not caused by something they had done or neglected to do.* I was determined throughout my career to remove the burden of guilt that only added to the anguish of parents who were doing their utmost to help their children improve despite their overwhelming developmental disorder. During all the years that psychoanalytic thinking dominated psychiatry, parents became the scapegoats on whom the onus of guilt was heaped. Meanwhile, interest was being stifled in biochemical research, which was to give us many valuable guidelines for alternative therapies that *would* be effective.

Parents, relatives, friends, and some professionals were pleased to see the steady improvement of children who had seemed hopeless. Within three to six months, these children on the orthomolecular program began to understand and obey commands. They showed a willingness to cooperate with parents and teachers, and their hyperactivity began to subside.

SCHIZOPHRENIA

Schizophrenia is a complex and varied syndrome. Seldom, if ever, do patients have all the symptoms, but most have many of them. Common to all schizophrenics are altered perceptions, emotions, thinking patterns, and sense of time. Many "hear voices" and have feelings "too strong" or "mixed up"—anxiety, fear, panic, depression, inability to concentrate, impaired short-term memory and recall, fatigue, insomnia, and thought disorder. Schizophrenics can be argumentative, negligent, forgetful, and destructive. They are likely to have more anxiety than depression, and they are prone to withdraw from others. The schizophrenic child may complain or even threaten his parents or professionals if they do not provide immediate relief for his suffering. "I have cancer of the nerves," a young schizophrenic said of her disease.

The genetic component of schizophrenia is substantial, but our culture continues to hold that parents bring on this affliction in their children in some psychodynamic way. It is a corollary of the old "nature versus nurture" controversy. Part of the blame can be laid at the door of Freud and his colleagues. They theorized that all psychiatric illnesses had their origin in early life experiences. But even the founder of psychoanalysis lived long enough to revise his thinking and to speculate that schizophrenia would become susceptible to biochemical treatment sometime and that research would "one day blow away the psychodynamic superstructure of mental illness."

As one of the pioneers in orthomolecular medicine, I discovered that many schizophrenics needed an intake of vitamins not provided in the normal diet in order to achieve the optimum molecular environment for their minds. Again, these are not vitamin deficiencies in the conventional sense; that is, a lack of those needed to nourish the body. To bring their brain chemistry into balance, these very sick people can take as many as 40 grams of vitamin C a day before there is any "spillover" into the urine.

If, as I am fully convinced, schizophrenia is indeed genetically predisposed, it should be shared as a "family affair." The suffering member deserves the concern of the whole family. Compassion, not shame or fault-finding, should be his due.

73

Dr. Cott's Help for Your Learning Disabled Child

An informed society would be supportive of parents of very sick children instead of blaming them as causative agents.

My success with the orthomolecular approach has been corroborated by scores of other doctors throughout the country who have used the same techniques to help these extremely ill children. Within weeks after treatment begins, parents gratefully report that their child has begun at least to sleep well. Sleep irregularities are among the more agonizing features of this disease; they aggravate the distress of the sick child, who then interrupts the sleep of the entire household.

As treatment progresses, I sometimes elevate the dosages to levels substantially higher than I prescribe for milder learning disabled children. For brief periods I will administer megadoses of vitamins B_3, C, and B_6, and I have never observed any serious side effects. Within a few months, these are among the changes that routinely occur:

1. Hyperactivity eases.

2. There is an end to the perpetual ritualistic movements of hands and arms and the explosive screaming and hollering.

3. A positive attitude develops about getting well and carrying out instructions.

4. A child will acquire certain accomplishments, such as being able to dress himself and tie his shoes, play by himself in the yard, and make tentative moves toward friendships. For him, these are giant steps.

5. He begins to smile appropriately at times, to hum tunes, and to regain any speech lost after the on-

slaught of the illness. Many children develop the
gift of laughter and a strong sense of hygiene and
personal grooming.

Until quite recently, it was believed that schizophrenia did
not occur among children under the age of ten. We know
better now. It can be suspected and diagnosed in the early
months of the life of the infant. Confusing schizophrenia with
retardation in the very young is a consequence of the traditional
practice of diagnosing the symptom rather than the disease.
This is why schizophrenia has been labeled WBD—the
wastebasket diagnosis.

With young children, it is difficult most of the time to
detect a clear and obvious personality change. We know something is wrong when a child inexplicably begins to fail in school
and is unable to keep up with his classmates, but alteration
in personality is the one important *constant* characteristic of
schizophrenia.

Schizophrenia beginning early in life is potentially the most
harmful. There is always the chance that the illness will disappear spontaneously, but early detection and treatment offer
the best hope of staving off a lifetime of misery. Schizophrenia
can be most devastating when it surfaces shortly after the child
has begun to speak. Verbalization of thought processes may
stop altogether. Youngsters who have learned a few words seem
unable to learn more words, and they often forget the words
they do know. Should the disease recede, the degree of speech
recovery depends on how long the child was ill.

Some of the senses of schizophrenic children are altered. The
world of these children is not at all like the world of other
children. These children suffer distortions in perceptions of
time, space, vision, hearing, even of their own bodies. Their
characteristically intense hyperactivity may in part be due to

75

their distorted way of experiencing time. The repetitive questioning in which almost all such children engage also reflects this anomaly in time perception. The few seconds they wait for the answer to their question may seem like an eternity to them. Time becomes so distorted that the days seem to have no end. To help detect this dyschronia, I use a metronome with an auditory and visual input to learn more exactly the nature of the time distortions, and then I know pretty well how "fast a track" a particular child is on.

Years ago, I discovered that the improvement in my young schizophrenic patients was often even more remarkable than that of most of the adult schizophrenics I was treating. From the beginning, I concurred with Linus Pauling that the provision of optimal concentration of substances normally present in the body offered the best start-up treatment available to schizophrenics. Only after significant gains have been made can any other therapy (if indicated) prove meaningful.

To be specific, let me recount a personal experience:

I am going to tell you briefly about a boy named Billy. He was an extremely disordered boy. I came to know him well, and I still keep in touch with him.

At the age of two, Billy was excessively hyperactive. He talked like a speeded-up tape recorder and would bang his head on the headboard of his bed. He cried constantly. When he was three, he began to reject all food. The tranquilizers prescribed by his pediatrician only "drove him out of his skin." Interestingly, his intellectual curiosity was beyond his years. But his vocabulary, which had been quite large, began to diminish when he was five. He showed no developing independence. He learned to read, write, and do arithmetic. But he lived in a private world untouched by the presence of others.

By the second grade, Billy was being taunted by his classmates, and this brought on temper tantrums. He forgot how to do things he had been doing for a long time, such as tying his shoelaces; a year later, his attention span became even shorter and his schoolwork deteriorated. He was diagnosed as having schizophrenia.

Three times a week, during the years that Billy was ten and eleven years old, he spent an hour consulting with a psychiatrist. This doctor ultimately recommended that Billy be placed in a residential school or a day school that accommodated children with problems similar to his.

Billy thought he was becoming crazier and crazier. He was consumed by hopelessness. To be without hope is the consummate tragedy, and he begged his parents to destroy him.

"Kill me, kill me, kill me!" Billy screamed. "For God's sake, kill me! I don't want to live and I can't do it myself. I am useless, hopeless. Oh, please, please, mother, kill me!"

A friend of Billy's mother happened to see me on a television talk show discussing the orthomolecular approach as it applied both to very sick children and to shadow children. This friend seemed particularly impressed when I spoke of the possibility of schizophrenia occurring as the result of a biochemical disorder and mentioned that elevated dosages of certain nutrient substances can help to correct the disorder.

During his first visit to my office, Billy retreated behind chairs and paced like a trapped animal clawing to escape his prison. He threatened to become "like Hitler and destroy the world and everything in it" if no one helped him. I told his parents that treatment would be ongoing for years, and I was guarded in my prognosis because Billy was already twelve years old.

Billy made no noticeable gain in the first months of treatment. He continued to speak poorly and to act strangely, and he was always about to "climb the walls." But when I was able to double the dosages, there was a radical change in his behavior. He began to speak with his parents in a completely clear and normal manner, with none of the usual repetitions, hesitations, nonsense, and oddities of expression. His topics were sensible, and he no longer talked about dying or getting even with the world.

There were setbacks. Billy became ill, and his father berated Billy's mother and accused her of poisoning Billy with "those damn pills."

I should say in passing that when there are "dropouts" from the orthomolecular treatment, the blame is usually not put on the prescribed dosage per se. More culpable is the daily effort of eating this and taking that, and it all becomes "too much hassle" for the child or for both parents and child. At this point, I reduced Billy's dosage temporarily, then brought it back to full strength. Billy improved even more. The boy began to respond differently to his parents and to his environment. He seemed to be breaking through the darkness that had imprisoned him for so long. He was in a state of shocked reality. Everything was all new, and sometimes terrifying, to him. He tried to balance himself emotionally, with one foot in each of his two worlds, not knowing whether to step forward to the new, expanding world or backward into the old, confining one, where at least he knew his way around. I told his parents that many of my patients have similar problems as they become healthier. This was indeed a trying time for Billy because of the stimulation to the brain that comes with orthomolecular therapy.

Billy had been seriously overweight when he first came to see me, and I said emphatically that he must lose at least thirty pounds. As he lost weight, treatment worked more effectively. He could not keep up with his changing mental patterns. I thought that perhaps he was progressing too rapidly and that his body was pushing him in a direction for which he was not prepared emotionally. So I stopped all medication for a while and gradually reintroduced several components of the treatment.

Billy had been in and out of various schools. Now he entered a private psycho-educational school offering a personal, involved relationship therapy. He learned to defend himself when attacked. He no longer begged for help with his schoolwork. He stopped complaining about noise and loudness, and his hypochondria disappeared. He joked; instead of fantasizing about Hitler, he developed a taste for Laurel and Hardy movies. He had control over his daydream world and the changing concept of himself. He played games like the other boys, and he no longer thought something was wrong with his brain.

"We had tried all the conventional psychological methods of treatment, with fruitless results, before using vitamins," Billy's mother wrote me. "I believe that without the vitamins we would have lost our son forever. I say this unequivocally; nothing could convince me otherwise. How do I feel about orthomolecular medicine? How does one feel about a gift from God?"

Today, Billy is in his late twenties. He has been doing clerical work for a number of years in an electronics laboratory in New Jersey. His mother describes him as kind and thoughtful and loving, more patient and more sociable as the years go by, generous to a fault, and self-assertive.

Rejecting those professional opinions that would have placed the blame for Billy's severe affliction on the "errors" they had made during his early life, his parents sought help for an illness they had become convinced was of biochemical, not psychological, origin. Their search led them into the world of biochemistry, where there have been great breakthroughs in the understanding and the treatment of the very ill.

Many traditional physicians, at the insistence of parents, are agreeing at least to administer the orthomolecular regimen. Before prescribing megadosages of vitamins, some of them will conscientiously read the literature and consult doctors experienced in this approach. But there are those doctors who will report that their "experiment" was a failure. I have personally looked into some of these "failures." What I find is that the doctors have tried the discipline and abandoned it before it had a chance to be effective. Or they had given timid, "watered-down" dosages. This approach, it bears repeating, is a long-term treatment. It can take months—and mountains of patience—before there are discernible signs of progress in very sick children.

Every year that passes, tens of thousands of young people are developing schizophrenia. About one-third of these youngsters are gravely harmed for the rest of their lives. The remarkable safety of the orthomolecular therapy should make its use obligatory if we go by the stricture that anything that is harmless and possibly effective should be tried. Two-thirds of the people who develop schizophrenia return to hospitals for periods of time ranging from a few weeks to several years. At least half of these incapacitated cases, in my reckoning, could be restored to acceptable functioning levels if treated with vitamins and minerals.

I also feel strongly that young people who are otherwise doomed to be in and out of mental hospitals for most of their lives should have certain rights that are normally not within the purview of average children. One such right is to demand a type of treatment that might be successful, even though it goes against the medical advice the family may be receiving.

Schizophrenia has been with us since the beginning of mankind and has not changed noticeably through the ages. At best guess, it attacks one out of every one hundred people throughout the world. I have observed patients with schizophrenia from such far-flung lands as England, Australia, India, Nepal, Iran, Iraq, the Soviet Union, and Argentina. The disease differs from country to country only in its delusional content, which is influenced by the particular society and its culture.

Although much work and much research are still required to fill the remaining gaps in our knowledge of childhood schizophrenia, there is reason for encouragement in the successes being achieved by orthomolecular medicine in the three decades that it has been applied to this dreadful disease. New discoveries in biochemistry constitute a revolution likely to be as decisive in the history of the next one hundred and fifty years as the Industrial Revolution has been in the last hundred and fifty years. With schizophrenia and other psychoses proving susceptible to supernutritional approaches, it would seem that we already have a futuristic approach to the control of this wasteful, heartbreaking illness.

AUTISM

So inspired was I by my results with schizophrenic children that I extended the orthomolecular approach to treatment of other psychoses of childhood, principally to autism. Autism, like schizophrenia, is the result of a metabolic disorder; the overlapping symptoms of the two illnesses are manifestations of perceptual distortions. I believe that these distortions may come from disturbances in the brain chemistry and the improper molecular concentration of certain essential vitamins and other nutrients in the cells of the brain.

Autism, which occurs in one out of three thousand or so infants, is a severe disorder of behavior, learning, and communication. The developmental disability of an autistic child interferes with the growth of his cognitive functions; that is, those functions of the brain by which we learn. This child rarely develops speech beyond echoing what he hears. Ask him, "Do you want some milk?" and he will answer, "Do you want some milk?"

Autism is not defined by origin or cause but by a collection of associated symptoms or behaviors. The autistic child tends to live in a dream world. He is oblivious to everything around him. (The word *autistic* comes from the Greek word for "self.") His brain power, vision, and hearing may not be defective, but he cannot communicate with others. He is self-absorbed in such activities as lint-catching, thread-pulling, blanket-sucking, circle-walking, toe-walking, bed-bouncing, jumping around, spinning and rocking, closing doors, and babbling incoherent messages. He is fascinated with inanimate objects but demonstrates no anticipatory gestures when being approached or picked up by family members, and he has an aversion for physical contact. He is obsessively withdrawn.

Dr. Bernard Rimland and his colleagues have demonstrated conclusively that many autistic children—as well as autistic adults—benefit markedly from large amounts of vitamin B_6 and magnesium.

In numerous examinations carried out at the Children's Brain Research Clinic in Washington, D.C., it was discovered that more than 50 percent of autistic children showed abnormal uric acid levels and widespread abnormalities in calcium metabolism. It was determined that there was a greater incidence of thyroid disease and a greater incidence of exposure to chemicals in the history of parents of autistic children prior to conception as compared with parents of the control children. There were also more gastrointestinal problems in both autistic children and their parents.

"When you have an autistic child," one distraught father has said, "you have ten children. The little son of a bitch demands so much and gives back next to nothing." He confessed that there were times when he fantasized about killing the child before the child killed him and his wife; he was enormously relieved to learn that other parents with autistic children shared this ghoulish daydream.

The tragic fate of most of the hundred thousand or more autistic children in this country will be to end up sooner or later in institutions described by one embittered parent as "Potemkin villages." During visiting days, such institutions take on the facade of respectability, cleanliness, and caring. But in essence they are little more than human warehouses.

This is a bleak projection. Autistic children are improvable. And in improvement lies their hope for a sweeter destiny.

As the autistic child begins to respond to the orthomolecular approach, he has awareness for the first time of the real world around him. He begins to react in some measure to other people. He makes tentative efforts toward speech. First, there is an intelligible word or two, and the words grow into phrases; the quality of speaking improves. He becomes loving, and can not only endure cuddling but seeks it. Gradually, he acquires a taste for new and wholesome foods. One parent, in her exhilaration, exclaimed, "This is like Lourdes!" Heretofore, some of these very sick children have been fruitlessly exposed to every form of treatment: operant conditioning, steroid injections, adrenocortical extract, patterning, psychotherapy, electroshock, music therapy, tranquilizers, sedatives, and amphetamines. Now at last something is "taking hold."

Here are thumbnail sketches of two autistic children who improved through the orthomolecular approach:

Lydia B., at the age of three months, had a *Candida albicans* yeast infection, a detriment to her normal development. At two, she was speaking well and able to count to twenty, but she did not use language to communicate. Presently, she began

83

to lose her vocabulary. Eventually, she stopped speaking altogether. She did a lot of yelling. She would not chew and she would bloat after eating. Food had to be ground up for her. I first saw her some weeks before her fourth birthday. Two months after orthomolecular treatment began, Lydia was eating better and had learned to chew. As her treatment progressed, she became more aware of what was going on around her and she developed eye contact. Teachers in her kindergarten commented on her remarkable gains.

Christopher E. was four years old when his parents brought him in for a consultation. He continually opened and shut his jaws, grinding his teeth. He was totally uninterested in all things and people in his environment. Some months after treatment began, his parents reported substantive improvements. Christopher became interested in playing with his toys. He recognized a variety of shapes. Speech was just beginning, and he was communicating realistically with gestures.

DOWN'S SYNDROME

Of all the gross alienations of the newly born, none is wreathed in more dread and feelings of hopelessness than Down's syndrome. It occurs in approximately one out of every one thousand births. It is a mutation of chromosome 21. The incidence of Down's syndrome births is higher among women who are more than thirty-five-years old when they have their first child. Women are also at greater risk if they had hyperthyroidism prior to conception or during early pregnancy or if they had some viral infection, such as hepatitis, or if their history includes several miscarriages. These women seem to share a vitamin B_1 deficiency—a deficiency that could be corrected before conception and throughout pregnancy.

At one time, the parents of a Down's syndrome child were

stigmatized for having produced a "mongoloid idiot." In this congenital birth defect, the epicanthal fold of the upper eyelid accounts for the somewhat Oriental, or mongoloid, appearance. Other distinguishing signs are cranial and facial abnormalities, such as a flattening of the back of the head, simian palmar creases, and short fingers and toes. There is injury to the functions of the entire body: digestion, absorption of nutrients, and elimination of waste. Some children become severely retarded. Speech impediments are common, and IQs range from the thirties to the fifties. By the time Down's syndrome children are two or three years old, they are already a year or more behind normal children, and their development in the areas of exercise, speech, and socialization is slowed.

Everything in my experience has made me hopeful about Down's syndrome children. If they cannot be brought into normal maturation, they can at least secure a place for themselves where they can function to their potential with dignity. With increasing nutritional awareness, we can anticipate a time when there will be fewer instances of this disability. For those afflicted, there will be an extension of life expectancy during which there will be an increasingly normal maturation of the central nervous system and of the skeletal system, improved motor skills, and more easily controlled behavior.

No success that I have had with orthomolecular medicine has pleased me more than the improvements I have seen in my Down's syndrome patients, and I have treated some who were as young as ten months. It is nothing short of thrilling to see some of these seemingly hopeless youngsters begin to develop skills in reading, writing, and arithmetic and become coordinated enough to engage in sports activities.

Medical science may not yet have found ways to extend significantly the lifelines of these most sorely afflicted of children. But so much can be done to open up their eyes and hearts and minds to the wonders of the world around them for however long they do live. There is no need for a Down's syndrome child to remain imprisoned within incapacities wrongly regarded as "frozen."

An illustrious example of this hopeful prognosis is the story of Jonathan V., whose continuing progress is such a source of satisfaction to me.

I first saw Jonathan when he was seven years old. He had the typical facies of a mongoloid child. There was a simian fold in both of his hands, which showed the ability to hyperextend. His voice was hoarse and what speech he had was garbled almost beyond comprehensibility. Jonathan was the youngest of four children; his mother was forty-one years old at the time of his birth.

I recall that I put Jonathan on a daily regimen of quite a few substances. I advised his taking brewer's dried yeast tablets; niacinamide; vitamins B_6, B_{12}, C, and E; calcium pantothenate; dolomite tablets; chelated zinc; calcium pangamate; folic acid; and chelated manganese.

A year or so later, his mother called to report that Jonathan had been off his "medicine" for six months. She thought he was "improving." He was growing and gaining weight, but he *was* undisciplined and hyperactive, and his speech was still garbled. I told her to resume giving him everything I had prescribed.

"Jonathan is reading!" his mother exclaimed when next I heard from her. "And writing! And he's speaking ever so much better. Jonathan is *learning*, Dr. Cott!"

Jonathan had gotten off to a delayed start. But at twelve years of age he could read "anything" and was continuing to progress. He had been in the second grade with normal children, had made As and Bs in all his subjects, and was promoted to the third grade.

In the fourth grade, Jonathan was given an equivalency test and scored in the 75th percentile. That was also the year he was confirmed, and I was pleased and touched to receive from him a handwritten invitation to his bar mitzvah. How well he read from the Torah in Hebrew!

Jonathan is now nineteen and is doing very well in a mainstream high school. His speech is clear. He has many friends and confides to me that some of them are girl friends.

In the early 1970s, I was invited by the president of the Alabama Schizophrenia Foundation, Glenn Ireland, to speak on the orthomolecular approach to the treatment of schizophrenia. I reported that my successful results with these severely disordered children had time and again been duplicated by many other doctors following my procedures.

The idea began to germinate in the minds of Mr. Ireland and his wife, Mallie, to establish a school in Birmingham for very sick children. In Alabama, schizophrenic and autistic children were excluded from academic programs in the public schools. There were no special education classes in the public school system and no private schools for these children, either. Funds were raised principally through the zealousness of the Irelands to establish a school for these neglected youngsters. In appreciation of my counsel—and of my consent to play a supervisory role in the administration of treatment and the development of the curriculum—the school was named in my honor.

The Allan Cott School opened in Birmingham in September 1974, with an enrollment of eighteen students. Today, it accommodates more than fifty. Most of our students are placed on the megavitamin, mineral, amino acid, and diet program. Parents are cooperative in administering the regimen and in enforcing especially the restriction on sugar and foods prepared with sugar. Those students whom we discover to be sensitive to milk or who have symptoms of celiac disease are maintained on a specialized diet. The youngsters are assigned to classes compatible with their needs and abilities. Weekly staff conferences facilitate continual revision in the goals for each student.

Emphasis at the school centers primarily on the following areas:

1. Behavioral—developing techniques and disciplines that decrease and discourage inappropriate and undesirable conduct

2. Communication—increasing communicable skills, whether they be verbal, sign, or symbolic

3. Functional living—training in self-help, self-direction, leisure-time behavior, and home tasks

4. Vocational—the teaching of work-related tasks and work conduct

5. Functional academics—the adaptation of academic tasks into daily activities

As the children progress in the development of functional living skills, much of the burden of their care is lifted from the shoulders of their families. Classes are small and structured, and they are conducted in an atmosphere of love and acceptance.

The abiding creed of the school is that *every child has the right to learn.* Each child must be allowed to learn to his full potential within the framework imposed by only his own developmental limits. A diagnosis should not be used to exclude any child from education.

The greatest reward for the staff and for me is seeing how

many of our students are able to graduate from our school and enter into classes for less disturbed youngsters or occasionally into mainstream education.

The Allan Cott School began as a dream—a dream of concerned individuals that there could be a place for autistic, schizophrenic, and other severely disturbed children to learn and to grow. This school and schools like it are a beginning. We need so many more of them if countless thousands of seriously impaired children are to be rescued from the grim future otherwise awaiting them.

Chapter IX

Dietary Control and Allergies

As you can gather from the sampling of my case files in Chapter VII and from much of the foregoing text, I place the utmost importance on good nutrition and on the drastic alteration of the diets of the learning disabled children under my care.

"It is not enough for you to administer the vitamins and minerals I have prescribed and administer them in the indicated dosages," I tell a parent during the initial consultation. "Your other major responsibility in helping your child get better is to pay the closest attention to his diet. I will give you lists of allowable foods and those that must be strictly eliminated from his diet. If we should discover, as treatment progresses, that the child has any specific food allergies, those foods will have to be eliminated, too."

I cannot emphasize too strongly the fundamental role that diet plays throughout the life of every human being—from the moment of conception until that person draws his last breath. It is heartening, therefore, to note that today's mothers-to-be are not only increasingly aware of the necessity of a good diet but also are alert to the habits and substances that are noxious to them—the foremost of these being caffeine, alcohol, tobacco, and drugs.

"We are what we eat" no longer refers to our physical being only. It applies to our mental health as well. The state of our nutrition goes beyond affecting our moods and behavior; *it affects our very sanity*. Before this century ends, the need to relate the advances in the nutritional sciences to mainstream medicine will be accepted standard procedure. Until the present time, medical thinking and teaching have adhered to the narrow focus of nutritional deficiency diseases and have missed the importance of diet in the creation of an optimal molecular environment for the mind. Future generations will be the benefactors of the growing awareness that nutrition operates on all levels of biochemical and metabolic functioning.

Once the child is born, he can be truly well fed by most parents in this country. Even people in the most modest circumstances can afford to eat nutritiously. In fact, I repeat, it is more economical to eat well in the nutritional sense than to eat poorly. Compare the cost of a bowl of homemade oatmeal with the cost of a candy bar or a bag of potato chips, let alone a franchise burger with fries. The grocery bill for the average family is significantly inflated because of expenditures on the quick and easy—and nutrient-shy—foods.

Parents are less than exemplary when they take a casual attitude toward what their child is putting into his body. Each year, about five hundred new food products are introduced into the marketplace. Most of these items, I say without equivocation, are of negligible nutritive value. Food processors are permitted to use about three thousand additives; certain ice creams, for instance, contain as many as twenty additives. When children stuff themselves with non-nurturing and chemically loaded foods, they are exposing themselves to physical, mental, and emotional disabilities.

Dietary Control and Allergies

The National Nutrition Survey undertaken by the Department of Human Services reported an unexpectedly high prevalence of symptoms associated with severe malnutrition among the children they examined. One-third of the subjects under six years of age had anemia, and 17 percent showed abnormally low protein levels in their blood. Vitamin D—so necessary for the absorption of calcium and for bone development—was woefully lacking in many of the children. There was an astonishing incidence of rickets. Many, but by no means all, of the children were from the lower economic strata. Whatever the circumstances, the situation is deplorable. A child's body must grow and develop; a child's brain cannot wait for "better times." (More than incidentally, *only one person in a thousand* is free of every form of nutritional deficiency, according to the Bulletin of the Foundation for Nutrition and Stress Research.)

I am not in agreement with Vicki Lansky, author of *The Taming of the C.A.N.D.Y. Monster.* (C.A.N.D.Y. is an acronym for Continuously Advertised Nutritionally Deficient Yummies.) She holds that it is virtually impossible to prevent youngsters from filling up on junk foods. "Impossible," like "never," is a polarization well worth avoiding. I personally have known many a child who likes fruits and vegetables and who has no particular craving for candy or cola drinks. But if a child has not been conditioned in his earliest years to develop a taste for natural foods, a crucial change in eating habits may be difficult to attain.

There are hopeful signs. Parents are taking measures to rid the schools of the vending machines that purvey unwholesome foods and beverages. There are schools with enlightened lunch programs that feed children fresh fruits and vegetables and homemade soups and whole-grain breads. And young students are getting sound nutritional training from informed teachers.

The validity of parents as role models is no more strongly

demonstrated than in the pattern they set for eating habits. Too many children see their parents bolt down breakfast "on the run," and at the end of the day snack on pretzels or potato chips as they drink cocktails prior to eating TV dinners or a pizza or fried chicken from a "take-out" concession. Jane E. Brody, a health-news reporter for *The New York Times,* has used a personal experience to illustrate how a good parental example can be set. Her twin sons watched her as she carefully trimmed the skin off the chicken on her plate. The boys wanted to know why she was doing it. She explained that half of the fat of chicken is in the skin. What's wrong with fat? they asked her. She told them that while a certain amount of fat is essential to the diet, most people consume far too much of it, and this excess can lead to serious health problems. The next time she served chicken, she saw the boys cutting the skin off their servings, too.

"Your child *must* have a good breakfast," I exhort the parents of my young patients. "His brain cells must be adequately nourished to start him on his learning day. The best way to see that he eats this good breakfast is for you to sit down and share it with him. This may mean getting up a little earlier or starting preparations the night before, but a good breakfast need not be a major production." (Please see "Primer on Nutrition" for recommended meals, pages 199–218.)

I am reminded of the classic *New Yorker* cartoon of fifty years ago. At an elegant dinner table, the mother explains to her daughter that the dark green vegetable on their plates is broccoli. The spunky little kid rejoins, "I say it's spinach, and I say the hell with it."

Vegetables of any kind may be a "hard sell" to some children, but a wise parent will have the kind of nutritional information at hand that makes vegetables or any other desirable food enticing to the child. "The spinach, darling, is full of vitamins and iron that you need for the energy for skipping rope and doing all the other kinds of things you like to do."

A parent can become a "sneaky" cook and add nutrients to the foods a finicky child likes if he continues to protest that he doesn't want this and won't touch that. Vegetables, for instance, can be ground up for filler in meat loaf. There is hardly a child who doesn't like pancakes, and those pancakes can be highly nutritious if they are made with whole-wheat flour and with such supplements as chopped dates or nuts or raisins. And why not try weaning a child away from the beef or pork frankfurters and to the more nutritious, less fatty, less caloric chicken "hot dogs"?

I reserve my greatest grievance for foods and beverages containing cane sugar. Sugar is an insidious ingredient, and I applaud the mother who told me she had painted a skull and crossbones on the canister for sugar in her home. Sugary foods and beverages are bad for all children, learning disabled or not. In caring for my young patients, I find that a significant percentage of them improve dramatically when sugar alone is eliminated from their diet.

Sugar is like a firecracker. It agitates the brain chemistry and incites the explosive behavior classified as hyperactive. What happens is that the pancreas is overstimulated by sugar and secretes an overabundance of insulin, which reduces the sugar level in blood to a below-normal level. Unless there is a proper level of sugar in the blood, the brain cannot function efficiently. Constant overconsumption of sweets can undermine the mechanisms regulating blood sugar levels, and this upset leads to overactivity, irritability, poor concentration, attention deficit, and poor memory, among many other symptoms. With such symptoms, a child may be suffering from hypoglycemia.

Hypoglycemia is a condition brought on by an insufficient amount of glucose (sugar) in the bloodstream. It is commonly known as low blood sugar. There are those who regard hypoglycemia as no more than a trendy catchword to describe vague symptoms that elude proper diagnosis. But hypoglycemia is only too real, and it is much more prevalent than many physicians believe. Any doctor, in my opinion, who does not find at least two or three cases per thousand live births is probably missing them. Among premature births, the rate is forty-three per thousand.

Hypoglycemia results, then, from an overstimulation of the pancreas. Besides foods and beverages containing sugar, this overstimulation can come from any of the refined carbohydrates. (Refined carbohydrates, in the main, consist of foods made from any form of sugar or of products derived from white flour, such as bread or pastas. These foods are quickly converted to glucose and should be used sparingly, if at all.) The most common symptoms of hypoglycemia are recurring bouts of depression, anxiety, irritability, insomnia, exhaustion, fatigue, light-headedness, and vertigo. Some hypoglycemics manifest periodic episodes of violent, aggressive behavior.

Eating pasta with beans or rice with beans slows the conversion of the pasta or the rice to glucose, and the entry of the glucose into the bloodstream is slow, resulting in a slow rise of the sugar level. A slow rise is desirable, but a rapid rise of the sugar level overstimulates the pancreas and is best avoided.

Quite early on, I became aware of the role hypoglycemia plays in the creation of symptoms that were being recognized only as signs of anxiety neurosis (fatigue, recurring depression, irritability, headaches, and other neurological-like symptoms). So I began to perform glucose tolerance tests and found a high percentage of the patients were positive for reactive hypoglycemia or some other disturbance of glucose or insulin metabolism. I immediately removed all foods and beverages containing sugar and caffeine and other foods known to overstimulate the pancreas, and I prescribed specific vitamins, minerals, and a high-protein, low-carbohydrate diet.

The brain function of the hypoglycemic child is impaired. Even if he does not suffer from a learning disability, he will not learn as well as he should. The maintenance of a proper blood sugar level is essential to achieving the best molecular environment for the mind.

I have seen some children react to the withdrawal of sugar from their diet with a personality change and physical agony that resembles nothing so much as an addict going "cold turkey." These children, during this transitional phase, may also be subject to headaches and abdominal pains. Happily, there is almost always a marked improvement in behavior, performance, and temperament when the sugar-free diet has been in effect for even a brief time. If a child whose behavior has improved reverts to outbursts and temper tantrums and irascibility, I immediately suspect that he has found his way back to something he should not be eating—probably a sugary food or drink. One fifth-grader who would secretly eat cherry popsicles developed a phobia about going to school; when the popsicle habit was discovered and broken, the phobic behavior stopped.

I have had self-justifying parents contend that babies are born with a sweet tooth. No baby is born with a sweet tooth. The taste for sweets is acquired. A child will not clamor for "more cookies" unless that child has been fed cookies. I am not saying that children should not enjoy the usual fare of cake and ice cream at birthday parties. But sweets should be for that special occasion and not a staple of the daily menu. A parent should be able to find a tactful way of telling doting grandparents to forego the "goodies" and to bring some other kind of present. A parent certainly can choose a pediatrician who does not stock his waiting room with lollipops and Tootsie

Rolls. A child allowed to persist in gratifying his sweet tooth is on the way to developing an addiction to sugar and to a diet disastrously weighted by pastries, sugar-coated cereals, soft drinks, chewing gum, and candy.

Salt, too, is a learned yearning. If children are not fed over-salted food—and if they do not have before them the spectacle of parents dousing their food with salt before even tasting it—they are unlikely to crave salty foods later. Salt is an excessive ingredient in such junk foods as pretzels, crackers, pickles, hot dogs, and luncheon meats, as well as in most canned soups. Junk foods, to use a simplistic definition, are those foods relatively high in calories—an undesirable element in most instances—and relatively low in nutrients, which contain non-health-enhancing ingredients (saturated fats, sugar, salt, and devitaminized flour, in particular).

Parents, in lamentable naiveté, persist in believing that any food or beverage not forbidden by the Federal Food and Drug Administration must be at least noninjurious, if not wholesome. Parents should bear in mind that a child's health is affected by *everything* he eats and that their involvement must be aggressive and positive. They must go beyond depriving the child of things that have been labeled dangerous. It is their responsibility to provide him with an optimal diet. That optimal diet is one that contains a balance of quality protein, carbohydrates, fat, fiber, vitamins, and minerals.

At the "institutional" level, I am impressed with the nutritional benefits coming the way of some children in this country who would otherwise be permanently disadvantaged and underachieving. Take the Salem Children's Villages, to cite one example. These "villages," which originated in West Germany twenty or more years ago, function as homes for abused and abandoned children. They offer a natural environment for children who were residents of—or were headed for—

institutions or psychiatric hospitals. The children come under the care and guidance of professional "house parents," relief parents, and other trained staff people who administer to their needs in a familylike setting.

Nutrition is the primary facet of a multilevel program for modifying the behavior and personality problems of emotionally disturbed children and adolescents. Refined foods are not available there. Instead, there are fresh fruits and vegetables and homemade whole-grain breads. Desserts are either fruit or goods baked without sugar. Foods with chemical additives, especially salicylates, are never served. The diet is classified as natural food, lacto-ovo vegetarian. The Salem Children's Villages are situated in rural settings, and much of the food is grown on the premises.

A regimen of natural foods with their higher level of quality nutrients usually corrects many of the behavioral difficulties. *The Journal of Orthomolecular Medicine* described the experience of one twelve-year-old girl who entered a Salem Children's Village after living in a series of institutions. She had been diagnosed as hyperactive and possibly retarded, and was being maintained on large dosages of amphetamines, which she would wash down with tumblers of a sugar-ridden soft drink. The amphetamine habit exerted its usual appetite-depressant effect. The Salem Children's Village immediately began decreasing the medication and gradually withdrew it totally. The girl was placed on a diet free of junk food, and within months many of her behavioral and learning problems were reduced and her hyperactivity disappeared. With improved motor coordination, she learned to run and to swim. Her intellectual performance rose steadily. Without the dietary control, there is no doubt that she would have remained on medication and in an institution for the rest of her life.

In the U.S., there are Salem Children's Villages in Rumney,

New Hampshire (Box 56, Stinson Lake Road); Pittsboro, North Carolina; and Frostburg, Maryland. There are three in Germany and one each in Israel and Uganda.

As a corollary to the knowledge—and the enforcement—of good eating habits, parents must become sensitive to the prevalence of food-related allergies in their youngsters.

So many pale, tired, wheezing, itching, nervous children have been brought to me by anxious mothers suspecting some deep psychological disturbance, only for me to discover upon testing that the child's symptoms stem from an allergy.

The word *allergic* has entered into the mainstream vocabulary and is used loosely and often inaccurately. Not every wheeze or sneeze points to an allergy. Nor should parents be taken in by an artful dodge like, "If you make me eat that asparagus, I'll break out in hives and die."

An allergy can be described as an infection of modern times that has become almost epidemic as more potentially allergenic substances are introduced into the environment—and especially into the food and beverages we consume. Beyond the sensitivity to the chemicals in our environment, any one of the wholesome foods that are the basis of our daily meals can produce symptoms that can be recognized as stemming from an allergic origin.

At the same time, we must distinguish between food allergies and food sensitivities. If your child eats a dish of fresh strawberries and immediately there is a flushing of his skin, rashes, itching, and reactions in his ears or nose or throat, we are defining an allergy. But if symptoms such as minor joint and muscular pain, some depression and lethargy, a fairly painful or lasting headache, and upper and lower gastrointestinal malaise do not occur until many hours after he ate the dish of strawberries, we can say he has a food sensitivity. Nearly all of us have some sensitivity to one or more foods, but only a small percentage of us have a real food allergy.

If a parent brings in a two- or three-year-old who has been having rather chronic earaches, I suspect the child has a food allergy, a yeast sensitivity, or both. These earaches, if uninvestigated, may disappear when the child reaches the age of four or five. They will not disappear if they are due to a yeast sensitivity until that condition is treated successfully. If there is an allergy, it will later find another way of manifesting itself. More often than not, it will be in muscle ache or in back pain.

Any substance in the environment is potentially allergenic. It can be the budding lilacs in May, a papaya, cats, an old woolen sweater, fumes from the paint in a quartz heater, or even the plastic of a telephone receiver. Inside the average home there may be from twenty to one hundred and fifty chemicals in circulation.

Specifically, an allergy is a hypersensitivity causing the body to react to a substance known as an allergen. This reaction results in the formation of an antibody. When the antibody and the allergen react with certain cells, chemicals producing the symptoms of allergy are released. Millions of us, including children from the age of infancy, are susceptible to allergens.

The most pervasive of these allergens are the pollens produced by trees, grasses, and weeds. They cause the most common of all allergic reactions—hay fever. (Hay fever, incidentally, is a misnomer, because hay is not the irritant and there is no fever.) Recently, medical science isolated a chemical that is produced by the body during an allergic reaction to pollen and similar irritants. Thus we can hope that within a few years there will be on the market a vaccine for hay fever.

Molds and fungus spores growing in abundance on wheat, oats, corn, grasses, and leaves are other major allergens. Pollens and molds are relatively seasonal. But there are such all-seasonal allergens as dust, feathers, animal hairs, and animal dander (from dogs, cats, horses, and so on). It is the chemical allergens, however, that are being identified in ever-growing numbers. These are so prevalent in our foods and beverages, in our aerosol sprays, pesticides, carpet sprays, paints, varnishes, tobacco, perfumes—in felt-tip pens, inks, and mimeograph paper, bringing havoc to even brilliant students—that they become almost impossible to pinpoint. They are called "the great masqueraders," because they so easily escape detection. And even when they are identified, they are hard to avoid because they are being used so widely.

Children are particularly vulnerable to this chemical bombardment. Their adaptation mechanism decreases with constant exposure or with stress or fatigue; proportionately, their susceptibility increases. It is easy to see a relationship between allergies and mental symptoms or learning difficulties. The brain is the most sensitive organ in the body, and it is agitated by eating or drinking the "wrong" substances. Food-related allergies malign the nervous systems of millions of children. These allergies explain much mysterious fatigue, systemic aches and pains, and erratic behavior. These less obvious symptoms are far more commonplace than rashes, hives, wheezing, sneezing, or seizures, and they signify an allergy at work.

An allergy may cause one child to "act up" and another to be laid low with lethargy. Or within the same child there may be enormous swings in mood from listlessness to high excitability. Extreme mood changes should tell a parent that something is wrong. Symptomatic, also, of the presence of allergy are bloating, frequent headaches, and dark circles or puffiness under the eyes.

A quantum leap forward to the aid of hyperactive children was made by the discovery of their allergic reaction to the artificial colorings and flavorings they were consuming in food and beverages. (I am confident that a consensus is forming that these additives must go, and I doubt that anyone except the manufacturers will grieve for their elimination from processed foods.) At the same time, we learned that a large variety of fresh fruits and vegetables containing substances called salicylates could be antagonistic to many children—foods such as apples, oranges, peaches, tomatoes, grapes, cherries, strawberries, cucumbers, and green peppers.

The list of allergenic foods by no means ends with these foods and all the sugar-laden foods and drinks. Now we know that milk is by no means "the perfect food" for all children. Breast milk may be the *ne plus ultra* in an infant's diet, but cow's milk can be blamed for the high incidence of abdominal discomfort, earaches, obesity, and mucous formation in young children, as well as specific allergic reactions. Millions of children—including a majority of black children—cannot tolerate cow's milk or products made from cow's milk. These children lack the enzyme necessary for the digestion of milk. Furthermore, homogenized, fortified milk contains BHT and BHA—antioxidants added to protect the vitamin A—and some children have bad reactions to these compounds. One acceptable alternative to cow's milk is lactose-treated milk, which contains the enzyme product lactaid. Goat's milk and milk made from soybeans are splendid substitutes. It is fortunate that we have these milk variations for allergic children, because milk is an excellent source not only for protein but for other essential nutrients: phosphorus; potassium; riboflavin; and vitamins A, B_{12}, and D. The most crucial of milk's nutrients for growing children, as we all know, is calcium, the mineral necessary for strong bones and good teeth.

Besides certain fruits, vegetables, and milk, there are other foods some allergic children cannot eat at all. Among them are eggs, corn, chocolate, and any product made from wheat.

DR. COTT'S HELP FOR YOUR LEARNING DISABLED CHILD

Testing for food allergies has been discontinued by many allergists because in the past the only available method for testing was the skin test. The skin test is reliable as a test for inhalant allergens but was found to be unreliable for food allergies and quite unpleasant for children. Nor could adequate treatment be based on the results. There are, of course, within the medical profession many practitioners who specialize in all types of allergy discovery and treatment. Introduced recently was a test concentrating exclusively on food allergies. This "cytotoxic" test purports to identify an individual's possibly allergenic reaction to any of 186 potentially offending foods and beverages. It also claims to measure the severity of reaction on a numerical scale ranging from 1 (least) to 4 (most). This test is still controversial, but at least it aims toward comprehensiveness, and patients of mine have been helped through the findings. A copy of the cytotoxic test appears on pages 108–110.

Most of my young patients whom I suspect of being allergic to certain foods and/or beverages will respond to the elimination (allergy-finding) diet I suggest and not require testing services or visits to allergy specialists. When in consultation with the parents we seem to have discovered the offending foods and/or beverages, I urge that they be removed from the diet. Quite rapidly, we notice an improvement in the behavior of the child. Within a week or so, his hyperactivity decreases. This progress is the more remarkable in view of the fact that it takes the human system—and this applies to everyone—*four* days to rid itself of the last vestiges of any solid food.

I know from years of observation that the foods or beverages most likely to be allergenic for a particular child are those he consumes in the largest amount and for which he may have a real craving. So I make these foods and/or beverages the starting point for the elimination diet that I supervise. When a child

104

tells me that no day goes by without his drinking two or more cans of some sweet, fizzy drink, I know exactly what must be struck first from his diet.

The foods and beverages that even very bright children consume can make them seem dull or stupid and create the hyperactive behavior roadblock to learning. The removal from the diet of any beverage, including milk, consumed in one-half gallon amounts daily, usually results in dramatic improvement. My condemnation of sugar as the number-one offender has the corroboration of many parents and teachers alike. A mother will tell me that a birthday party with the inevitable sweets invariably triggers "off the wall" behavior. Teachers will call in "sick" the day after Hallowe'en to avoid the shenanigans of students who were overly "treated" the night before.

I have seen allergy-related difficulties drop reading levels by several grades, handwriting become childish and irregular, and instances of mirror-imaging (that is, writing backward). If parents suspect that a food allergy may be at the root of the child's baffling behavior or deteriorating schoolwork, they should try to find a pediatrician who is knowledgeable about allergies. Procedurally, that doctor should initiate an elimination diet in order to identify the offending food or foods the child is consuming. If the parents do not have access to a doctor with this expertise, let me suggest a few steps that they can take on their own and that they may want to discuss with the child if the child is old enough.

1. Observe your child closely for a few days. Keep a list of what is going into his system. Note his activities and the symptoms from day to day.

2. Delete every likely offending food or beverage from

the diet. I suggest you start by scratching all sweets and sugary foods and beverages from his diet, as well as other foods with artificial colors and flavors. Read the labels on all packaged foods.

3. Try to keep forbidden foods out of his reach. The best way to do this is to stop bringing them into the house.

4. Be calm in the face of any withdrawal symptoms—headaches, fatigue, irritability—your child may experience on this elimination diet. These reactions probably reflect his craving for—even his addiction to—the foods that are being eliminated.

5. Continue the regimen for up to three weeks. Try to monitor what your child is consuming away from home so that he is not "sneaking" any proscribed foods or beverages.

6. Watch for improved behavior. At such a time, an eliminated item can be returned to the diet each day (barring anything containing sugar, of course), but if there is a negative reaction—and this would occur within a day—you know that you have discovered at least one source of your child's allergy. That food must be omitted from his diet for an indefinite period. If it is a wholesome food and is again introduced, it should not be used more often than every fourth or fifth day.

7. Repeat the test with the suspect food to make sure it is indeed setting off the bad reaction. You do not want to take away from your child any wholesome food unless it really is allergy-provoking.

Dietary Control and Allergies

Genetically and biochemically, the children of today are astonishingly different from the children of thirty years ago—the generation of their parents. Much has entered into the total environment of children that did not exist in the 1950s. So much of the medical literature has become obsolete that the doctor examining a child for allergies is better off relying upon direct observation rather than upon textbooks.

The knowledge of nutrition and wise eating habits is too vital to be entrusted to the writers of television commercials whose aim is to peddle, not to educate. That education should be coming from the medical profession. But it is my sad observation that the average physician is not nutrition-oriented.

The good news is that more and more young people coming into the medical profession *are* nutrition-conscious. The new breed of doctors recognizes that nutrition education should be centered on foods: their specific composition and caloric value, and the interrelated roles they play in advancing our well-being. The new people in medicine also know this information must be passed along to all people in a way that communicates its importance.

CYTOTOXIC TEST

The cytotoxic test determines the source or sources of an allergy or a food sensitivity. Sources based on a blood sampling range from a mild sensitivity (1) to a severely allergic reaction (4). Ideally, any positive response should cause elimination of that food or beverage from the diet. (The Cytotoxic Test is a creation of Physicians Laboratories, Inc., of Los Angeles, California, Doug A. Kaufmann, President.)

REACTION 1 2 3 4	FOODS
	Banana
1 ☐ ☐ ☐ ☐	banana
	Beech
2 ☐ ☐ ☐ ☐	chestnuts
	Bellflower, Thistle
3 ☐ ☐ ☐ ☐	artichoke
4 ☐ ☐ ☐ ☐	lettuce
5 ☐ ☐ ☐ ☐	safflower oil
6 ☐ ☐ ☐ ☐	sunflower oil
	Berch
7 ☐ ☐ ☐ ☐	filbert
	Brassica
8 ☐ ☐ ☐ ☐	broccoli
9 ☐ ☐ ☐ ☐	Brussels sprouts
10 ☐ ☐ ☐ ☐	cabbage
11 ☐ ☐ ☐ ☐	cauliflower
12 ☐ ☐ ☐ ☐	kale
13 ☐ ☐ ☐ ☐	radish
14 ☐ ☐ ☐ ☐	turnip
	Buckthorn
15 ☐ ☐ ☐ ☐	grape, raisin
	Buckwheat
16 ☐ ☐ ☐ ☐	buckwheat
17 ☐ ☐ ☐ ☐	rhubarb
	Carica
18 ☐ ☐ ☐ ☐	papaya
	Carrot
19 ☐ ☐ ☐ ☐	caraway
20 ☐ ☐ ☐ ☐	carrot
21 ☐ ☐ ☐ ☐	celery
22 ☐ ☐ ☐ ☐	parsnip
	Cashew
23 ☐ ☐ ☐ ☐	cashew
24 ☐ ☐ ☐ ☐	mango
	Cereal Grains (grasses)
25 ☐ ☐ ☐ ☐	barley
26 ☐ ☐ ☐ ☐	cane sugar
27 ☐ ☐ ☐ ☐	corn (maize)
28 ☐ ☐ ☐ ☐	corn gluten
29 ☐ ☐ ☐ ☐	corn sugar
30 ☐ ☐ ☐ ☐	hops
31 ☐ ☐ ☐ ☐	malt
32 ☐ ☐ ☐ ☐	millet
33 ☐ ☐ ☐ ☐	oats
34 ☐ ☐ ☐ ☐	rice
35 ☐ ☐ ☐ ☐	wild rice
36 ☐ ☐ ☐ ☐	rye
37 ☐ ☐ ☐ ☐	wheat
	Composite
38 ☐ ☐ ☐ ☐	endive
	Cyperaceae
39 ☐ ☐ ☐ ☐	water chestnuts
	Bony Fish
40 ☐ ☐ ☐ ☐	bass
41 ☐ ☐ ☐ ☐	catfish
42 ☐ ☐ ☐ ☐	cod
43 ☐ ☐ ☐ ☐	flounder
44 ☐ ☐ ☐ ☐	halibut
45 ☐ ☐ ☐ ☐	herring
46 ☐ ☐ ☐ ☐	mackerel
47 ☐ ☐ ☐ ☐	mullet
48 ☐ ☐ ☐ ☐	perch
49 ☐ ☐ ☐ ☐	red snapper
50 ☐ ☐ ☐ ☐	salmon
51 ☐ ☐ ☐ ☐	sardine
52 ☐ ☐ ☐ ☐	smelt
53 ☐ ☐ ☐ ☐	sole
54 ☐ ☐ ☐ ☐	swordfish
55 ☐ ☐ ☐ ☐	trout
56 ☐ ☐ ☐ ☐	tuna
	Cartilaginous Fish
57 ☐ ☐ ☐ ☐	shark
	Crustaceans
58 ☐ ☐ ☐ ☐	crab
59 ☐ ☐ ☐ ☐	lobster
60 ☐ ☐ ☐ ☐	shrimp
	Farinosa
61 ☐ ☐ ☐ ☐	pineapple
	Fungus
62 ☐ ☐ ☐ ☐	baker's yeast
63 ☐ ☐ ☐ ☐	brewer's yeast
64 ☐ ☐ ☐ ☐	mushroom
	Ginger
65 ☐ ☐ ☐ ☐	ginger
66 ☐ ☐ ☐ ☐	turmeric

Dietary Control and Allergies

REACTION 1 2 3 4	FOODS
	Gourd Order
67 ☐☐☐☐	cantaloupe
68 ☐☐☐☐	crenshaw melon
69 ☐☐☐☐	cucumber
70 ☐☐☐☐	honeydew melon
71 ☐☐☐☐	pumpkin
72 ☐☐☐☐	squash (summer)
73 ☐☐☐☐	squash (winter)
74 ☐☐☐☐	watermelon
	Heath
75 ☐☐☐☐	blueberry
76 ☐☐☐☐	boysenberry
77 ☐☐☐☐	gooseberry
	Honey-suckle
78 ☐☐☐☐	cranberry
	Laurel
79 ☐☐☐☐	avocado
80 ☐☐☐☐	cinnamon
	Legume
81 ☐☐☐☐	alfalfa
82 ☐☐☐☐	bean (kidney)
83 ☐☐☐☐	bean (lima)
84 ☐☐☐☐	bean (mung)
85 ☐☐☐☐	bean (pinto)
86 ☐☐☐☐	bean (soy)
87 ☐☐☐☐	bean (string)
88 ☐☐☐☐	black-eyed pea
89 ☐☐☐☐	carob
90 ☐☐☐☐	chick pea (garbanzo)

REACTION 1 2 3 4	FOODS
91 ☐☐☐☐	lentil
92 ☐☐☐☐	pea
93 ☐☐☐☐	peanut
94 ☐☐☐☐	split pea
	Lily
95 ☐☐☐☐	asparagus
96 ☐☐☐☐	chives
97 ☐☐☐☐	garlic
98 ☐☐☐☐	leek
99 ☐☐☐☐	onion
	Madder
100 ☐☐☐☐	coffee
	Mulberry
101 ☐☐☐☐	fig
	Mallow
102 ☐☐☐☐	cottonseed
	Mammals
103 ☐☐☐☐	beef
104 ☐☐☐☐	butter
105 ☐☐☐☐	calf's liver
106 ☐☐☐☐	cheese (American)
107 ☐☐☐☐	cheese (bleu)
108 ☐☐☐☐	cheese (cottage)
109 ☐☐☐☐	cheese (mozzarella)
110 ☐☐☐☐	cheese (parmesan)
111 ☐☐☐☐	cheese (provolone)
112 ☐☐☐☐	cheese (Swiss)
113 ☐☐☐☐	cow's milk
114 ☐☐☐☐	lamb
115 ☐☐☐☐	pork
116 ☐☐☐☐	yogurt

REACTION 1 2 3 4	FOODS
	Maple
117 ☐☐☐☐	maple sugar
	Mollusks
118 ☐☐☐☐	abalone
119 ☐☐☐☐	clam
120 ☐☐☐☐	oyster
	Mustard
121 ☐☐☐☐	collard greens
122 ☐☐☐☐	mustard
	Myristiceae
123 ☐☐☐☐	nutmeg (mace)
	Myrtle
124 ☐☐☐☐	clove
	Nightshade
125 ☐☐☐☐	eggplant
126 ☐☐☐☐	paprika
127 ☐☐☐☐	chili pepper
128 ☐☐☐☐	garden peppers
129 ☐☐☐☐	potato
130 ☐☐☐☐	tobacco
131 ☐☐☐☐	tomato
	Nightshade—Mint
132 ☐☐☐☐	peppermint (spearmint)
133 ☐☐☐☐	sage

REACTION	FOODS
1 2 3 4	
	Night-shade— Morning Glory
134 ☐ ☐ ☐ ☐	sweet potato (maroon) yam
135 ☐ ☐ ☐ ☐	sweet potato (yellow)
	Night-shade— Pedalium
136 ☐ ☐ ☐ ☐	sesame
	Orchid
137 ☐ ☐ ☐ ☐	vanilla
	Palm
138 ☐ ☐ ☐ ☐	date
139 ☐ ☐ ☐ ☐	coconut
	Parsley
140 ☐ ☐ ☐ ☐	watercress
	Pepper
141 ☐ ☐ ☐ ☐	black pepper
	Pink
142 ☐ ☐ ☐ ☐	beet
143 ☐ ☐ ☐ ☐	beet sugar
144 ☐ ☐ ☐ ☐	spinach
145 ☐ ☐ ☐ ☐	swiss chard
	Poultry
146 ☐ ☐ ☐ ☐	chicken
147 ☐ ☐ ☐ ☐	chicken egg white

REACTION	FOODS
1 2 3 4	
148 ☐ ☐ ☐ ☐	chicken egg yolk
149 ☐ ☐ ☐ ☐	duck
150 ☐ ☐ ☐ ☐	goose
151 ☐ ☐ ☐ ☐	pheasant
152 ☐ ☐ ☐ ☐	turkey
	Rose
153 ☐ ☐ ☐ ☐	apple
154 ☐ ☐ ☐ ☐	apricot
155 ☐ ☐ ☐ ☐	blackberry
156 ☐ ☐ ☐ ☐	cherry (prunus)
157 ☐ ☐ ☐ ☐	nectarine
158 ☐ ☐ ☐ ☐	peach
159 ☐ ☐ ☐ ☐	pear
160 ☐ ☐ ☐ ☐	plum, prune
161 ☐ ☐ ☐ ☐	strawberry
	Rue
162 ☐ ☐ ☐ ☐	grapefruit
163 ☐ ☐ ☐ ☐	lemon
164 ☐ ☐ ☐ ☐	lime
165 ☐ ☐ ☐ ☐	orange
166 ☐ ☐ ☐ ☐	tangerine
	Sapucaia
167 ☐ ☐ ☐ ☐	brazil nut
	Spurgel
168 ☐ ☐ ☐ ☐	curry
169 ☐ ☐ ☐ ☐	tapioca, cassava, yucca
	Sterculia
170 ☐ ☐ ☐ ☐	cocoa, chocolate
171 ☐ ☐ ☐ ☐	cola nut

REACTION	FOODS
1 2 3 4	
	Tea
172 ☐ ☐ ☐ ☐	tea, black
	Walnut
173 ☐ ☐ ☐ ☐	pecan
174 ☐ ☐ ☐ ☐	walnut
	Other
175 ☐ ☐ ☐ ☐	allspice
176 ☐ ☐ ☐ ☐	almond
177 ☐ ☐ ☐ ☐	aspirin
178 ☐ ☐ ☐ ☐	food coloring
179 ☐ ☐ ☐ ☐	goat's milk
180 ☐ ☐ ☐ ☐	honey
181 ☐ ☐ ☐ ☐	horseradish
182 ☐ ☐ ☐ ☐	MSG
183 ☐ ☐ ☐ ☐	olives
184 ☐ ☐ ☐ ☐	oregano
185 ☐ ☐ ☐ ☐	saccharin
186 ☐ ☐ ☐ ☐	thyme
187 ☐ ☐ ☐ ☐	_____
188 ☐ ☐ ☐ ☐	_____
189 ☐ ☐ ☐ ☐	_____
190 ☐ ☐ ☐ ☐	_____
191 ☐ ☐ ☐ ☐	_____
192 ☐ ☐ ☐ ☐	_____
193 ☐ ☐ ☐ ☐	_____
194 ☐ ☐ ☐ ☐	_____
195 ☐ ☐ ☐ ☐	_____

Chapter X

Vitamins and Minerals

I CANNOT OVEREMPHASIZE the need for sufficient quantities of nutrients in the diets of *all* children. The consequences of vitamin deficiency among too many children—and not only among shadow children—are glaring and startling. Medical literature abounds with one unfortunate account after another. I shall cite a few examples in which corrected deficiencies brought about startling results.

Half of the slowest readers in a classroom were given vitamin supplementations of A, B_1, B_2, B_3, B_{12}, and D. The other half were given sweets. When tested, the vitamin group outperformed the children eating confections by an astounding 175 percent in reading and 35 percent in spelling, and they achieved a superiority of 6.7 IQ points.

In a controlled IQ study of 351 students, those children with higher levels of vitamin C in the blood scored an average of 5 points higher than those with a lesser C level. When those children with less vitamin C in their diets were given supplementary orange juice for six months, the IQ of each increased by 3.54 points.

In a study conducted at Old Dominion University, in Norfolk, Virginia, eleven vitamins and eight minerals were introduced into the otherwise unchanged diet of sixteen mentally retarded children. Pains were taken to avoid the kinds of criticisms leveled at other such studies; that is, that any reported elevations in IQ were due to increased attention, socialization, or training. "Our study initiated no change whatever in the schooling, socialization, or life-style of these kids," Dr. Ruth Harrell, director of the study, declared. Over an eight-month period, there was an average increase in the children's IQ of 16 points. Vision in general also improved—so much so that two children no longer had to wear eyeglasses. Four of the children were able to progress into regular (mainstream) school classes.

When I visited the Moscow City Psychoneurological Clinic for Children and Adolescents, I learned that the speech of a group of children who had been diagnosed as retarded improved significantly after they were given oral dosages of twenty milligrams of B_{15} three times daily. Previously, these children had displayed little interest in anything and were described as passive and lacking initiative. A month after the B_{15} treatment got under way, there was a dramatic turnaround; their mental state, intellectual activity, concentration, and interest in toys and games began to soar, and there were noticeable improvements in speech and vocabulary.

The word *vitamin* is accurately rooted in *vita*—the Latin noun for "life."

Webster's Third New International Dictionary defines vitamins as "any of various organic substances essential in minute quantities to the nutrition of most animals and some plants, acting in the regulation of metabolic processes but do not provide energy or serve as building units, and are present in natural foodstuffs or sometimes produced within the body." The Columbia–Viking Encyclopedia, somewhat more simply, declares that vitamins are "essential for growth and maintenance of normal body structure and function."

I would quarrel with the Webster definition that only minute quantities are necessary for nutrition. Vitamins indeed are present in foods only in minute quantities, but they are largely diminished by the time food reaches the table. Fresh vegetables, in particular, begin to lose their vitamin content the moment they are picked. In the mass marketing of vegetables, it can be a week or longer before fresh-picked produce even reaches the greengrocers' stalls. If vegetables are processed either through canning or freezing, they immediately lose a high percentage of their vitamins and minerals.

So more and more, as the distance between the grower and the consumer has increased—and food technology has progressed—we have had to turn to vitamin supplements. They are one kind of insurance protecting our nutritional needs.

Thus far, fifteen vitamins have been identified. I would not be the least bit surprised if there are not others awaiting discovery. So much have vitamins, however controversial, become a part of the general consciousness that many people are surprised to learn that they were first isolated only as recently as the second decade of this century (by the Polish-American biochemist Casimir Funk). Research into the identification and uses of vitamins is continuous and open-ended; there may be no more active area in the whole realm of medical investigation. As I write today, for example, researchers at Johns Hopkins University Hospital are establishing that the red blood cells destroyed by the consumption of alcoholic beverages can be resuscitated by vitamin B_6 supplementation.

Why, with all the convincing documentation of the benefits of vitamin supplements, is there still lingering antagonism toward their use? (Perhaps we should not wonder too much when even the august *Harvard Medical School Health Letter* has difficulty making a distinction between vitamins and drugs. In its September 1984 forum on learning disabilities, it states,

"Inappropriate drugs such as . . . megavitamins, are often pushed." *Drugs?*)

Those who deplore the attempts of many people to patch themselves up by taking vitamins on their own without having medical examinations or counsel are right. But these critics would be on firmer ground if they did not go to the other extreme of protesting that the average American need have no fear of dietary inadequacies.

The general public must be advised, admittedly, against self-imposed treatment with megadosages of vitamins or other nutrients, such as too much B_6 without complementary doses of B_2 and the rest of the B-complex vitamins. There exist many antagonistic reactions between vitamins and minerals, which can be avoided if these nutrients are prescribed by a knowledgeable physician. Vitamins unfortunately lend themselves to all sorts of unproven notions and "quick cures" and are used too often for self-medication in cases requiring skilled diagnoses and careful treatment.

Pediatricians who do not prescribe vitamin regimens may have little interest in nutrition or have not read the literature about the advances being made through the orthomolecular approach. A sufficiency of vitamins has healthful benefits to confer upon all children. Youngsters have fewer colds, earaches do not develop, sleep improves, sore throats occur more rarely, appetites perk up, and undersize children make growth spurts.

I never cease to be amazed by the number of people who can wax apoplectic at the suggestion of vitamin therapy but who will then unquestioningly take into their system any prescribed or unprescribed drug they are offered, not to mention all the harmful substances in their daily diet.

I happen to believe that the metabolic differences among individuals vary up to a thousandfold, because we are all biochemically unique and have unique requirements. Nutrition researchers in China, where diet has rarely been questioned, have also come to the conclusion that "what may be enough vitamins for you may not be enough for me."

When the antivitamin crusaders are not alleging the toxicity of vitamin supplements, they are asserting that vitamins do not do anything and reminding us that the vitamin industry is a billion-dollars-a-year business. What they do not know—or what they choose to ignore—is that a therapeutic, preventive vitamin regimen costs a fraction of what one pays for prescription drugs. To treat any number of quite commonplace physical ailments can cost hundreds of dollars a month in medication. In point of fact, so relatively unprofitable are vitamins that they have been called the "orphan medicine." (The Market Research Corporation of America has reported that people spend only about eight cents a day for vitamins.)

The needs of any individual can vary from one day to the next. A person under great stress may require many times the amount of the Recommended Daily Allowance of B vitamins. The same is true of minerals. After surgery, for example, the body loses considerable amounts of zinc; supplemental zinc becomes highly valuable in the healing process.

Vitamin supplements are either fat-soluble or water-soluble. The fat-soluble vitamins—A, D, E, and K—dissolve in fat and are more easily stored in the body. Inasmuch as water-soluble vitamins dissolve in water, they are much more easily lost by the body through the normal process of elimination. The principal vitamins used in orthomolecular medicine, the various Bs and C, are water-soluble.

VITAMIN SYLLABUS
(WITH SPECIFIC APPLICATION TO CHILDREN)

Vitamin A. It enhances normal growth of the young, builds new tissues, and protects against infection. It is essential for healthy skin, good blood, strong bones and teeth, kidneys, bladder, lungs, and membranes. (In adults, it may extend longevity and curtail the symptoms of senility.) A deficiency of vitamin A can result in poor night vision, insomnia, fatigue, depression, extreme nerve pain, and such birth defects as cleft palate and congenital impairments of the eyes and the heart. The Department of Agriculture points out that one person in four gets less than the Recommended Daily Allowance of 5000 IU of vitamins. (An IU, or international unit, is an amount such as any fixed quantity or measure used as a standard in medicine and not confined to measurement in any one country but used in all countries for the substance that is prescribed; in most cases, it is equivalent to a milligram.) Vitamin A is a derivative of carotinoid pigments of plants and can be made synthetically. Among its best natural sources are milk and other dairy products; fish-liver oils; carrots, squash, and other yellow vegetables; tomatoes; spinach, broccoli, and other dark green vegetables; cantaloupes, peaches, and other yellow fruits. The need for vitamin A increases during the winter in northern climates, because it is metabolized more slowly by the body in cold weather.

B vitamins. We call this group a "family," or complex, because they are found approximately in the same foods and perform similar functions in the body; a deficiency in one of the B vitamins is often indistinguishable from the symptoms of deficiency in another. Basically, the B vitamins are active in providing the body with energy by converting carbohydrates into glucose, which the body burns to produce energy. They are necessary for the metabolism of fats and proteins and are the single most important factor for the health and normal functioning of the nervous system. Furthermore, they are indispensable for the maintenance of muscle tone in the gastrointestinal tract and for the health of skin, hair, eyes, mouth, and liver. When the body is low on the B vitamins, we feel fatigued, depressed, tense, irritable, apathetic, confused, headachy, or stressful. All the B vitamins are natural constituents of brewer's yeast, desiccated liver and other organ meats, wheat germ, whole grains, brown rice, legumes, nuts, lean meats, poultry, fish, and leafy green vegetables. Brewer's yeast is the richest natural source of the B complex group. For many people, however, B vitamins derived from yeast are interdicted because sensitivity to yeast is widespread. The B vitamins are also produced by intestinal bacteria, which grow best in milk. Maintaining milk-free diets or taking antibiotics may destroy these valuable bacteria. All B vitamins are readily absorbed and any excess is excreted, but the vitamins must be replaced continually. In taking B complex in tablet form, those preparations that have all the Bs in the same quantity should be selected. If a tablet contains 50 mg. of B_1 (thiamine), it should also contain 50 mg. of the other vitamins in the B family— B_2 (riboflavin), B_6 (pyridoxine), niacinamide, pantothenic acid, choline, bitartrate, inositol, and para-aminobenzoic acid (PABA). B_{12} (cyanocobalamin), folic acid, and biotin are measured in microgram doses. B complex vitamins bear a relationship to one another, and to take some in selectively large dosages can result in a deficiency of others; a deficiency of B_2 occurs, for instance, when large dosages of B_6 are taken without supplementing the B_2. This deficiency may become manifest by the cracking of the skin in the corners of the mouth.

Vitamin B_1 (thiamine). Renowned originally for preventing beriberi, this vitamin is essential for keeping the nervous system in good operating order and for the maintenance of normal appetite, good digestion and carbohydrate metabolism, and for optimal maturation of the young. Any kind of stress—

including the stress of vigorous exercise—increases the need for B_1. Routine use of foods like white rice, white flour, white sugar, chocolate, alcohol, beverages containing caffeine, and tobacco contribute to a deficiency of B_1 because they diminish the body's store of this vitamin. Thiamine is a specific treatment for the subclinical beriberi symptom of neuritis and neuralgia occurring in chronic alcoholism. A clue to a B_1 deficiency may be a sensation of numbness or burning in the hands or feet. Aside from the usual sources of B vitamins, B_1 is also found in blackstrap molasses.

Vitamin B_2 (riboflavin). The American diet may be most frequently lacking in this vitamin. The earliest sign of a deficiency is usually cracks in the corners of the mouth. But if the deficiency is not recognized and it progresses, symptoms of skin lesions, damage to the eyes, trembling, dizziness, insomnia, mental sluggishness, and an increase in the cancer-causing potential of some carcinogens result. B_2 is important for good muscle tone, and it is conducive to the metabolism of protein, fats, and carbohydrates.

Vitamin B_3 (niacin or nicotinic acid or niacinamide). Credited with virtually eliminating pellagra in most parts of the world, niacin is effective in reversing sensory dysperceptions such as hallucinations, delusional thinking, and disturbances of mood and energy. Here again reliance on refined, high-carbohydrate foods accounts to a great extent for a B_3 deficiency; available niacin is exhausted in breaking down these sugars and starches. High doses of B_3 may have behavioral effects unconnected with its role as a vitamin; it is valuable in the treatment of senility and produces a sedative benefit for people with sleeping problems. It plays an important role in easing the effects of stress on the body. In research done on rats, niacin prevented the formation of stress-induced ulcers. (It is always wise to elevate the intake of the other B vitamins to the same level, though B$_3$ may be the only vitamin needed in such high dosages.) Three grams daily of niacin are most effective for reducing high levels of cholesterol. Large doses of niacin raise the level of uric acid in the body and could precipitate gout. Therefore, blood levels of uric acid should be checked repeatedly during the use of large doses of niacin. B$_3$ is rarely used in treating children, because for the initial two or three days of its use a feeling of heat in the body and a mild flushing of the skin are produced. The reaction begins fifteen to twenty minutes after the pill is swallowed and lasts for half an hour and then recedes. It recurs with successive doses and ends usually in the second or third day. The symptoms are due to niacin's vasodilating action and the release of histamine into the skin.

Vitamin B$_6$ (pyridoxine). It is essential for the utilization of proteins and fats and for the production of red blood cells and disease-fighting antibodies. A deficiency can cause nervous symptoms and convulsions in infants and can result in mental retardation. Large amounts of B$_6$ (always to be taken under the supervision of a physician) are helpful in controlling convulsions in infants as well as in treating both childhood and adult schizophrenia and autism. B$_6$ is also beneficial for adolescents with acne, for premenstrual tension, for some pregnant women who suffer from morning sickness, and for treating anemia that does not respond to iron supplements. Many Americans are likely to be deficient in this vitamin because of its wholesale removal in the milling of white flour. B$_6$ is prescribed for learning disabled children with speech problems. It is extremely valuable in controlling disturbed, disruptive behavior. It has an antidepressant effect and is important for its antistress effect. Besides the usual sources of B vitamins, B$_6$ is to be found in bananas.

Vitamin B$_{12}$ (cyanocobalamin) nourishes bone marrow, the body's blood cell factory. An insufficient supply of B$_{12}$ will contribute to pernicious anemia and neurological degeneration. It is a key nutrient for stimulating growth in malnourished, undersize children, in maintaining fertility, and in fostering the production of breast milk.

Folic acid. Biochemically intertwined with B$_{12}$, this vitamin takes its name from *folium,* the Latin word for "leaf," and was first identified in spinach and later found in most leafy green vegetables.

Pantothenic acid. Because of its salubrious effects on the adrenal glands, this B vitamin has come to be known as the antistress vitamin. Along with calcium, it relieves the tension of the powerful jaw muscles that set teeth to grinding during sleep. It gets its name from the Greek word *pantos,* meaning "everywhere," because it is to be found in nearly all foods.

Choline reduces the blood pressure of some hypertensives and is helpful in treating cirrhosis. It is part of a substance that transmits nerve impulses, and as such it can be helpful in treating Tardive Dyskinesia—a side effect of the long-term use of psychotropic drugs used in the treatment of schizophrenia and once thought to be an irreversible condition. (Tardive Dyskinesia manifests itself in oral and facial grimaces; tongue movements; and spasmodic contractions of the neck muscles, causing a rotation of the chin and a twisting of the head to one side.) Choline is a constituent of lecithin and aids in the utilization of fat.

Inositol has a mild antianxiety quality comparable to the effect of tranquilizers like Valium and Equanil. This B vitamin lowers cholesterol levels and blood pressure, and helps in the removal of fatty deposits in the liver. It is a safe, highly effective sleep "medication." Another source for this vitamin is citrus fruits.

Biotin. Biotin is distinguished mostly for its relationship to avidin, a protein in raw egg whites that seizes on it and makes it unavailable to the body. Most people, except those on antibiotics for a long time, can manufacture biotin in their intestines. There is evidence that some people have excessive needs for this "minor" vitamin, particularly babies with skin conditions and chronic diarrhea, and some pregnant women and nursing mothers. Biotin helps to synthesize amino acids and fatty acids and to form RNA and DNA. It is used specifically to treat certain common skin inflammations of infants. Happily, most diets are sufficient in biotin.

Para-aminobenzoic Acid (PABA). Really a vitamin within a vitamin (it is a component of folic acid), it aids in the utilization of proteins, fats, and carbohydrates, and is necessary for the formation of blood cells, especially red blood cells, and for hair pigmentation.

Vitamin B$_{15}$ (pangamic acid). This recently discovered vitamin has had the misfortune of enjoying a trendiness, which in itself is sufficient for critics to dismiss it as a fad and a substance of inconsequential value. It was first isolated from aqueous extracts of kernels of apricot stones, and later it was crystallized from rice shoots, rice bran, brewer's yeast, bull blood, and horse liver. Most of the basic research was done in the Soviet Union. A quite extraordinary achievement attributable to pangamic acid is the improvement in children with speech difficulties. (See case files at the end of this chapter for specific references to children with speech impairments who were treated successfully with B$_{15}$.) I believe the virtues of pangamic acid to be incontestable. Research in the Soviet Union has reported that large supplements of B$_{15}$ have helped more than 80 percent of patients suffering from cardiovascular disease. The controversial substance is also used to treat a vast number of disorders, which include alcoholism and other chemical addictions; autism and schizophrenia; minimal brain damage; and hypertension.

Vitamin C (ascorbic acid). Many of us esteem this vitamin as the most valuable of them all. There is considerable evidence that all people could benefit from supplements of vitamin C. C helps in the formation of the connective tissue in all cells. It helps to lower cholesterol and to enhance iron absorption. It aids in healing and in the production of red blood cells, and it is a tremendous boon to mentally ill adults and children alike who tend to have markedly atypical metabolisms insofar as the key nutrilites (vitamins, essential amino acids, minerals, fatty acids) are involved. Vitamin C's most fervent admirers, proclaiming its versatility, believe it can do everything from preventing the common cold to staving off cancer. We know that C is a detoxifier that reduces the toll of heavy metals, carbon monoxide, and sulfur dioxide polluting the air, and of many potentially malignant carcinogens. It has been found helpful in treating inflammatory diseases such as rheumatoid arthritis. A total deprivation of C would result in scurvy. Symptoms of this vitamin deficiency include tenderness and bleeding of gums, loosening of teeth, soreness of joints, weakness, fatigue, listlessness, and depression. Many an older person who is assumed to be senile—because of dazed or fuzzy responses—may only be in need of larger amounts of vitamin C (and niacin) to restore alertness. There is evidence that C also acts as a tranquilizer and as a sedative for insomniacs. Vitamin C is the one vitamin that man and other primates do not manufacture within themselves; they must get it from food. Our needs for C may be much higher than is generally assumed. Those animals that manufacture their own C do so in very high amounts; a 150-pound goat, for example, produces thirteen grams of it every day. (I know of professional men in their eighties and even nineties who are taking ten or more grams every day.) The most concentrated sources of vitamin C are the citrus fruits, but plentiful quantities are also to be found in tomatoes, parsley, peppers, leafy green vegetables, corn, and potatoes. Most commercial vitamin C tablets are derived from corn.

Vitamin D. A deficiency results in rickets, a common blight of urban youngsters living in areas where pollution blots out the beneficial rays of the sun. (D is created by sunlight acting on the oils of the skin.) This vitamin aids in the development of normal bones and tooth structure. It promotes muscle strength and helps regulate the heart through calcium absorption. In tandem with vitamin A, D has been employed to treat arthritis, chronic anxiety, and depression. Its principal sources are liver, egg yolk, sardines, herring, salmon, and fish-liver oil. It is now almost universally added to milk and other dairy products.

Vitamin E. An antioxidant, it is considered a booster for the heart because it has a beneficial effect on circulation. Ever since Drs. Evan and Wilfred E. Shute, of Canada, "popularized" this vitamin, the most extravagant claims have been made for its powers. It has been hailed as everything from the "sex vitamin" (a natural aphrodisiac) to a magical anti-aging substance that will keep us looking young and feeling fit forever. We do know that it inhibits the formation of blood clots and protects the lungs. It has been dubbed "nature's own tranquilizer" because of its soothing effect. A grievous lack of it in the diet does not occur often. But a serious deficiency is conducive to infertility, muscular dystrophy, and vascular abnormality. Alternate sources of vitamin E are most vegetable oils, brown rice, oats, raw nuts, cabbage, asparagus, leafy vegetables, eggs, meat, beef liver, molasses, and legumes.

Vitamin K. This is widely known as the "bloodclotting" vitamin, and it performs a role in the normal functioning of the liver. Its deficiency is most commonly found among elderly people, because so many of them in general subsist on poor diets or are on antibiotic medication. Too little K in the diet of infants, also a common occurrence, induces diarrhea, which is routinely treated with antibiotics, and this actually increases the K requirements in order to prevent bleeding problems. Vitamin K deficiencies can be ameliorated by increased intakes of tomatoes, egg yolks, lean meat, peas, cow's milk, yogurt, carrots, soybeans, blackstrap molasses, potatoes, leafy green vegetables, and polyunsaturated oils.

Vitamin P (the bioflavonoids). This vitamin could be called the handmaiden of vitamin C because it helps to prevent destruction of ascorbic acid by oxidation. There is evidence to suggest that the bioflavonoids, if consumed in adequate quantities, are helpful in preventing cataract formation. (Several years ago, I had the privilege of reading a letter written by Dr. Albert Szent-Gyorgyi, who was awarded the Nobel Prize for his discovery of vitamin C in 1932. The letter, sent to a colleague, stated that his research had convinced him that bioflavonoids have this preventive capacity.) Vitamin P is found in the same foods as vitamin C.

MINERALS

Although minerals are less publicized than vitamins, they are at least as important. They are crucial for nutrition and metabolism. Deficiencies turn out to be diagnostically significant. A trace mineral deprivation can induce bizarre behavior, such as depression or a state of hyperactivity. Conversely, conditions as severe as schizophrenia can often be alleviated with the supplementation of one or more minerals (zinc, manganese, and chromium). The amount varies according to the patient's needs.

Calcium. As any parent knows, calcium builds strong bones and teeth. It also has a becalming effect. It helps in normalizing blood clotting and is essential for rhythmic heart action. The most conspicuous source of calcium is milk and milk products. Whole grains, unrefined cereals, and green vegetables are excellent sources also, particularly for those youngsters (and others) who cannot tolerate dairy products.

Chromium aids in the breaking down of carbohydrates and also plays a role in the metabolism of glucose (for energy) and the synthesis of fatty acids and cholesterol. Chromium is present in unsaturated fats, meats, clams, brewer's yeast, liver, and whole grain cereal.

Copper. This trace mineral is necessary, too, for proper bone formation and the production of RNA. It also assists in the composition of hemoglobin and red blood cells. Copper occurs in liver, whole grain products, almonds, green leafy vegetables, and most seafoods. An overabundance of it can act as a toxic heavy metal. Copper builds up in the body when unusually large amounts of tap water are consumed daily. Use of birth control pills and other synthetic hormones and of antibiotics increases the level of copper. Zinc is a natural antagonist for excesses of copper in the body.

Iron is also essential for the production of hemoglobin. It builds up the quality of blood and improves resistance to stress and disease. Abundant sources of iron are to be found in liver, lean meats, eggs, whole grain breads and cereals, certain fruits and vegetables, and brewer's yeast.

Magnesium plays a vital role in the functioning of nerves and muscles and in the maintenance of healthy bones. It is a component of nuts, whole grain foods, dried beans and peas, dark green vegetables, and soy products.

Manganese is necessary for normal skeletal development, and it helps to maintain sex-hormone production and the utilization of proteins, carbohydrates, and fats. It nourishes nerves and the brain. Manganese is found in egg yolks, sunflower seeds, wheat germ, whole grain cereals and flour, dried peas and beans, brewer's yeast, and bone meal.

Phosphorus is also essential for the utilization of carbohydrates, fats, and proteins for growth maintenance, cell repair, and energy production. It aids in skeletal growth and implements tooth development, kidney functioning, and transference of nerve impulses. Meat, fish, poultry, eggs, whole grains, seeds, and nuts are the sources of phosphorus. In children, in the bone growth period of development, this mineral is elevated and does not return to normal adult levels until bone growth is completed.

Potassium. Our muscles, nerves, and heart all need potassium. This important trace mineral helps in maintaining the balance of the blood and works in conjunction with sodium to regulate the body's water balance. Potassium is obtainable in vegetables (especially green leafy ones), apples, oranges, whole grains, sunflower seeds, potatoes (particularly in the peels), and abundantly in bananas.

Selenium. Along with vitamin E, it works in metabolic processes and aids in normal body growth and fertility. Selenium occurs richly in bran, in the germs of cereals, and in broc-

coli, onions, tomatoes, and tuna. There is some evidence that
this mineral may have a cancer-preventive potential. Selenium
is also a mercury antagonist. In unusually large doses, it is a
toxic substance, which can produce an irreversible demye-
linating nerve disorder.

Zinc is essential for healing and the development of new
cells. It is an adjunct to enzymes in digestion and metabolism
and is vital to general growth, reproductive organs, and the
functioning of the prostate gland. Zinc is readily available in
oysters, brewer's yeast, bone meal, beans, nuts, seeds, wheat
germ, fish, and meat (especially liver).

VITAMIN B₁₅ CASE HISTORIES

Vitamin B_{15} (pangamic acid) was discovered, isolated, identified, and synthesized in the laboratory of E. T. Krebs, Sr.,
and E. T. Krebs, Jr., in San Francisco, in 1951.

B_{15} gives us a classic example of the difference between vitamins and drugs. A true drug is almost the exact opposite of
a vitamin. A true drug is toxic or at least irritative, stimulative,
or depressive in *any* dose. Vitamins, by contrast, can be consumed in elevated quantities without inducing negative reactions. Put another way, it is nearly impossible to have a
vitamin that is toxic or a drug that is non-toxic when each is
used within the boundaries of its optimal therapeutic response.

The scientific and clinical progress of vitamin B_{15} has been
characteristic of that of most important vitamins whose value
becomes increasingly apparent as research and clinical appli-
cations widen. This is in contrast to the history of all but a
few drugs. The ineffectiveness of most drugs grows increasingly
apparent as they are studied over the years. No vitamin has

ever come into clinical application without the scope of its usefulness becoming more and more undeniable.

The Soviet leadership in research in this newest of vitamins piqued my interest. I was particularly impressed with the results that Russian scientists were reporting with the use of B_{15} in the treatment of severely disordered children. In its work with children with speech difficulties, the Moscow City Psychoneurological Clinic for Children and Adolescents was a revelation to me, as I have noted. The patients showed considerable improvement after only one month of treatment with pangamic acid to the exclusion of all drugs.

On this encouraging note, I began supplementing my orthomolecular prescriptions with as much as 200 milligrams of vitamin B_{15} daily toward the goal of correcting or at least improving speech impairments. Emboldened by my success, I extended my application of B_{15} to treat other maladies that undermine a child's health and ability to learn—particularly those of asthma and allergies.

The following case files illustrate my experiences with vitamin B_{15}.

Gordon W.

Gordon was seven years old, emotionally disturbed, and had a vocabulary of five or six words when I started him on a daily regimen of 200 mg. of B_{15}. Within three weeks, his vocabulary had increased to include words such as *banana, chicken,* and *dinner,* and phrases such as *Get this.* He was constantly making sounds in the effort to communicate with others, and he developed an interest in playing games with his brothers and sisters. After three months Gordon was uttering a great many words and phrases, and his teacher observed that he *looked* different; he had the appearance of a "normal kid." As his treatment continued, so did the improvement in his speech. In a very short time Gordon made vast strides away from babyish ways and toward independence.

Oliver K.

This four-year-old had an almost immediate reaction to the vitamins: He became downright noisy, and his parents couldn't have been more pleased. He made sounds even in his sleep and he took to humming. He enjoyed hearing himself played back on the tape recorder. Within weeks he was able to say "Daddy" and "Mommy" clearly for the first time. A temporary exhaustion of the supply of vitamin B_{15} brought a regression to Oliver. He went from a peaceful, happy, easygoing child to one who could not sit still. He became terribly distressed, punching his baby brother every chance he got. His old symptom of head-banging returned. Three days after he was back on B_{15}, he was happy again and slept well through the night. A few months later, he was trying out new words every single day and using them appropriately. His mother told me that life with Oliver had become a joy. "It's the most exciting thing I have ever experienced," Mrs. K. wrote to me. "He answers questions now and he asks what's this and what's that and he knows the names of many things and he tells me them enthusiastically. He wears a big proud smile."

Joyce P.

Joyce was almost five years old when she came for treatment. At the beginning, she had some vomiting, so I advised her mother to discontinue temporarily all the vitamins except the B_{15}. Within several weeks Joyce was not only feeling better, she said two sentences. I advised that the B_{15} be increased and the other vitamins gradually reintroduced.

"The following three days were the most exciting I have ever known," Joyce's mother wrote me. "She spoke only in sentences, was eager to try everything, and was quick to respond. Neighbors and other children commented on the remarkable difference. Last Sunday, when Joyce was unaware of my presence, I saw her cover her naked doll with her coat as she said, 'That's all right, baby, I know you are cold. I will cover you with my coat and make you warm.'"

Elinor A.

I met Elinor when she was twelve. At the age of two and a half, she had been diagnosed as asthmatic. She had been given antihistamines, desensitization injections, and prednisone. She had missed at least half of one school year, and any physical exertion was beyond her.

The introduction of B_{15} was a turning point. During the spring and early summer, normally her worst months of the year because of the burgeoning vegetation, she improved steadily. She was able to dispense with the medications and to resume an active life of swimming, biking, and hiking.

Six months later, her mother reported that Elinor was virtually free of asthmatic attacks for the first time in her life. Elinor was becoming increasingly more active. She had taken up modern dance, and there was no wheezing or shortness of breath.

Stephan L.

Nine-year-old Stephan was brought to me by a mother who had all but given up hope of ever stopping his "croaking." He had had some success as a stage performer, but his asthmatic wheezing impaired his singing. He had great trouble recording; the tapes picked up his belabored breathing.

Weeks after he began vitamin B_{15} treatment, the story was quite different. Now Stephan could go out into any kind of weather without being bundled up to the eyeballs. He was playing basketball and bouncing up stairs with no breathlessness. He was in fine voice and recording without any of the asthmatic sound effects. His ecstatic mother dropped me a note saying, "I would like you to take another look at Stephan sometime next week to see for yourself the amazing recovery." I did see Stephan, and his recovery was indeed amazing.

Helen S.

Here is how Helen, who is now eighteen, summarized for me her successful orthomolecular treatment in which B_{15} was included:

"Before the B_{15}, I used to have coughing and wheezing attacks, which lasted from one to two-and-a-half hours. I would usually take my cough medicine and some hot tea and Medi-Haler to relieve them. These attacks used to occur two or three times a week. Since starting with B_{15}, I have had only one such attack, and it lasted for only half an hour.

"With the B_{15}, I have not wheezed once this year while exercising. For me it seems to have a preventive effect. It controls the asthma. Another advantage for me is that B_{15} does not cause an allergic reaction, which was not the case when I was taking an antihistamine. I feel so wonderful, and I can only attribute it to the use of B_{15}."

Richard R.

This ten-year-old was ridden with allergies. He had a breathing problem, especially when exposed to grasses, molds, ragweed, and other inhalants. His eyes would water and itch excessively.

The B_{15} relieved him almost immediately. But there came a time when he ran out of his supply and, sure enough, his old attacks returned. His parents gave him an antihistamine and injections for desensitization that were of minimal help. Once the B_{15} supply was replenished, Richard no longer had attacks, and he has had none since.

Melissa W.

She first came to my office when she was eleven, and her mother's subsequent letter speaks for itself:

"My daughter has been on B_{15} since you prescribed it last February. This was the first summer in all these years that she did not have a day of hay fever. If for any reason she does not have her B_{15} at hand for a couple of days or so, her behavior changes, and she is constantly angry. But with the B_{15} she is cooperative and appears to be alert, and she is free of agonizing symptoms. She is so improved in every way, but what delights her father and me most is that at last she is enthusiastic about school and is working there to the limit of her very considerable capacities."

Boris McG.

And another letter from a relieved parent, this one about two of his sons:

"Boris has become very cooperative, agreeable, pleasant, and willing. He has become inventive and shows a great deal of initiative. I don't know if any of this is due to the lack of school pressures or to his new participation in sports. But I trace all his improvement to the time he began taking B_{15}. At last he is a happy child. Ronald (Boris's brother) came home from a camping trip a couple of weeks ago with a cold and a slight attack of asthma. I gave him vitamin B_{15} twice a day. In one week, he was completely without symptoms, and he hasn't had any since."

Chapter XI

Coming into the World

VITAMINS AND MINERALS are a chapter in the autobiography of a child before he is even born.

You may recall the story of the distraught woman who visited the psychiatrist and asked him, "Doctor, please tell me how to have a healthy, normal child."

"Are you pregnant?" the psychiatrist asked her.

"Pregnant? My baby is seven years old."

"Oh, madam," the psychiatrist gasped, "you should have consulted me eight years ago."

The embryonic human being is the most neglected member of society today. Like Topsy, it just grows. When something goes amiss in the prenatal period—malformed heart, for instance, or an underdeveloped brain—society at large does not appreciate that there was a fetus struggling for air or fighting against infections or other dangers. Most of us accept at face value that the world has just another mentally deficient or maimed child.

What happens during the nine-month fetal period is far more important for the subsequent growth and development of the child than has been realized. From the age of antiquity, it was believed that if the embryonic child was safe, warm, and snug in his mother's womb, all was well. The fetus was being shielded and protected from all external influences while it floated in a fluid-filled sac insulating it from physical pressures. It was thought that the placenta acted as a barrier against the transmission of toxic substances from the mother's bloodstream. The awareness has come late that during these prenatal months this growing fetus is extraordinarily sensitive to its environment.

Part of the future of the baby-to-be depends upon the mother's immediate state of health. Above all, a pregnant woman's nutrition must be more than merely adequate; it must be the very best that circumstances allow. If she pollutes herself with drugs, alcohol, nicotine, or caffeine, she will be toxifying her unborn child. The fetus must be given the advantage of growing to term in an optimal molecular environment.

Each mother, by the diet she chooses, determines in large measure the type of baby she will have. In corroborating studies conducted at Harvard University and at the University of Toronto, it was found that no stillbirths occurred among mothers whose diets were more than merely adequate. When the pregnant women were eating well and not smoking cigarettes or drinking alcoholic beverages, birth was easier and babies were larger. Large babies are to be desired. Generally, they are healthier, brighter, less at risk to be learning disabled, and they are usually happier than smaller babies. A healthy diet also facilitates the nursing of an infant. Far more infections are found among babies whose mothers had poor prenatal diets.

Though deficiences in a pregnant woman's diet may not be conspicuous, they can severely affect her children with a multitude of diseases and psycho-physiological deficits. Nutritional privation during this period may retard both mental and emotional maturation. The child runs the risk of getting off to an unstable start and an insurmountable handicap in the critical years of its early development.

The period extending from conception to shortly after birth is an extremely vulnerable time. The negative prebirth factors, aside from faulty diet, include: bleeding during pregnancy; poor placental link to the uterus; induced labor; toxemia during pregnancy; infectious diseases of the expectant mother (German measles, a virus, influenza, or some chronic complaint); alcoholism or drug addiction; or Rh incompatibility.

Knowing as much as we do, it is lamentable that there has been a marked decrease in early prenatal care for pregnant women over recent years. The Children's Defense Fund, in noting this erosion of fetal nurturing, rightly calls it a "portent" of increased infant mortality as well as of a host of nonterminal distresses.

"Nor is birth an ending," as anthropologist Ashley Montagu observes. "It is more nearly a bridge between two stages of life, and although the bridge is not a long one, a child crosses it slowly, so that his body may be ready when he steps off at the far end."

Among birthing dangers are prematurity; induced labor; a long or difficult delivery producing anoxia; breech delivery; a poor fetal position; a dry birth (produced by premature rupture of the amniotic sac); intracranial pressure at the time of birth due to forceps delivery or a narrow pelvic arch; or a precipitous delivery that does not allow the plates of the skull to mold into the shape that permits the fetus to pass safely through the birth canal.

Possible postnatal hazards include delay in the beginning of breathing after birth (this is more common among premature babies, difficult deliveries, or twins); high fevers; sharp blows to the head from a fall or an accident; meningitis or encephalitis;

lead poisoning; drug intoxication; oxygen privation caused by suffocation, respiratory distress, or breath holding; severe nutritional deficiency; and the yeast infection known as *Candida albicans*, which weakens the immune system. When the suspected source of a learning disability occurs during the prenatal period, it is called *insult;* at birth, it is *trauma;* after birth, the term most often used is *damaged.* From the moment of conception until death, we are all subject to the possibility of brain damage.

In taking the detailed history of a learning disabled child, I ask the mother to describe her pregnancy. "Perfectly normal," I hear over and over again. I shudder when I contemplate some of these "perfectly normal" pregnancies. A mother will boast that she carried to full term without gaining a single ounce. Or she will casually speak of nausea and vomiting as if it went with the condition of being pregnant. Some of these women will look at me in astonishment and say, "Of course I was sick. I was sick every day with all three of my pregnancies."

As a result of poor diet, many women develop anemia during pregnancy. Others deprive themselves calorically at the behest of their doctor, who mistakenly believes that a small baby is preferable for an easy delivery. Amphetamines, routinely prescribed in the past to suppress appetite and to combat fatigue, only compound the developing problems. (Amphetamines are illegal and can no longer be prescribed except for treatment of a very rare disorder, narcolepsy, a sleeping sickness.)

Even mild caloric deficiencies in the diet of a pregnant woman can have serious consequences by the time her child reaches school age. Malnutrition in the early life of a child often results in reduced social responsiveness, a lack of interest in the environment, and low emotional development. Children who have a sound nutritional foundation during both the prenatal period and the first two years of life are far more active, involved, outgoing, and spontaneous than their deprived peers.

Severe malnutrition has a direct bearing upon infant mortality, crippling disease, and retardation of physical and mental development. It is not necessarily a reflection of poverty or parental ignorance. Some parents, taking the line of least resistance, allow their children to become "picky" or promiscuous eaters. Too many children use their allowances and lunch money to "graze," that is, to munch when and where they choose.

I would say to any expectant mother, "Your most important job is to take optimal care of yourself throughout your pregnancy. You are literally eating for two, breathing for two, and you should be partaking of the best—in the best sense of the word. You should be gaining weight during this period, and gaining it by eating fresh, whole, natural foods. I recommend fresh fruits and vegetables in quantity; nuts; seeds; and protein derived from fish, poultry, and vegetable sources rather than from animal or dairy products."

Babies undernourished in the uterus are scrawny, hypersensitive to any kind of stimulation, and likely to be fussy and troublesome. Shockingly, the mortality rate for babies born in the United States is considerably higher than that of those born in many other developed countries. There are eighteen other countries, in fact, that have fewer infant deaths per capita than does the U.S. One reason for this disturbing statistic is that so many babies here are born with less than desirable weights. Poor nutrition, alcohol and drug abuse, and teenage pregnancies are among the chief factors resulting in low birth weights.

The unborn child is a wondrous but fragile thing. Five to six weeks after conception, the face and the eyes of the fetus have taken shape. A severe jolt or a chemical change at that time may cause permanent damage. Lack of oxygen contributes to the greatest number of abnormalities.

The brain is the most vulnerable of the organs. It is irreversibly damaged if it is deprived of oxygen for even moments. Significantly, the brain is only a very small percentage of body weight, yet for it to function healthily a far greater proportion of nutrition is needed.

Between 6 and 8 percent of all births are premature, and premature births are the cause of 85 percent of infant mortality and of nonfetal complications among the newborn, such as respiratory distress syndrome. These tiny, fragile-looking infants also bring with them emotional unrest for their parents.

There are many conditions that put a woman at high risk for premature birthing. Among them are diseases of the liver, kidneys, and heart; a multiple pregnancy; a history of premature births or abortions; fetal malformations; premature rupture of the amniotic sac; pregnancies before the age of eighteen or after the age of forty; deficient prenatal care—as evidenced by poor nutrition, cigarette smoking, or consumption of drugs or alcohol; genital or other infections; eclampsia (high blood pressure) during pregnancy; small stature or poor physical condition, and any other undue physical or psychological stresses; placental abruption (premature separation of the placenta from the wall of the uterus); placental previa (location of the placenta in the lower part of the uterus, where it may become partially detached when the cervix dilates); a cervix that opens prematurely (a situation sometimes caused by multiple abortions); uterine malformation or fibroids; and prenatal exposure to the hormone DES.

"Pray for us now and at the hour of our birth," T. S. Eliot said aptly. Centuries earlier, another immortal poet, John Milton, wrote, in *Paradise Regained*, "The childhood shows the man, as morning shows the day."

The newborn child, under the best of circumstances, is a

wondrous organism. It knows a lot more than we commonly think it does. It sees more, hears more, comprehends more, and is predisposed to make friends with any adult who cares for it. It smiles, even if it is blind. It knows which sounds communicate, so it begins to imitate human sounds rather than the sounds of a television set or a whirring vacuum cleaner. It is extremely well coordinated and assembled for accomplishing the tasks of infancy—getting sustenance, maintaining contact with others, and defending itself against noxious stimulation. Its little ears begin to work while it is still in the womb, and after coming into the world it picks up more than had ever been suspected. It is a lip reader; it mimics adults' gestures; it exercises a variety of skills and actions that seem to come out of nowhere. It can tell the gender of other infants, and it prefers to look at babies of its own gender. We can only make one assumption: The newborn child has a mind. We might go on to assume that the genes carry the messages primitive humans needed for survival and that the learning of behavior patterns begins in the uterus.

Probably not more than one child in ten gets off to as good a start as he should. Indeed, that figure hardly seems radical in view of the facts that 13.5 million children in the United States live below the official poverty line, that nearly 7.5 million are currently on welfare, and that more than half a million babies are born every year to teenagers. Poor children are dying at a rate three times that of other children; poverty can be blamed for the death of 11,000 American children every year. In just a five-year period, that number adds up to more deaths than the total of American battlefield deaths during the ten-year Vietnam War.

Socioeconomic conditions are but one factor. The evidence accumulates that some drugs administered to pregnant women can cause behavioral abnormalities in their children. Obstetrical medications used in many hospitals may have long-lasting, deleterious effects on the emotional maturity of children born to these drugged mothers. Beyond questioning is the fact that chemically dependent mothers pass along their addictions to the newborn.

What to feed the newborn? No aspect of human life has been as subject to custom, superstition, ideology, and changing fashion. It was common in the American colonies to spoon into the mouth of an infant a paste consisting of butter, sugar, oil, and bread cooked in water; the baby was not allowed to feed on the first secretions from the breast, the colostrum, which we now know contains beneficial antibodies. Babies who survived the first day or so on that gruesome gruel were then nursed.

Breast-feeding is the earliest link in the immunological chain. The colostrum is rich in high-grade proteins and white cells, which the baby swallows to "seed" his intestinal flora. The healthy nursing mother experiences pleasure in the contact of breast and sucking mouth. A breast, the late Selma Fraiberg wrote, is "intended to bind the baby and his mother for the first year or two years of his life. If we read the biological program correctly, the period of breast-feeding insures continuity of mothering as part of the program for the formation of human bonds. A baby today experiences many more separations from his mother than the baby in traditional breast-feeding societies."

It is encouraging to note that breast-feeding has been increasing dramatically in recent years. Interestingly, it is the better-educated mothers who are more likely to breast-feed their babies. Bottle-feeding has declined accordingly, while the number of women who mix breast-feeding with bottle-feeding seems to have remained constant during the past decade.

"Breast-feeding is strongly recommended for full-term infants, except in the instances where specific contraindications exist," the Committee on Nutrition of the American Academy of Pediatrics has stipulated. The mother and her baby should remain together during the first twenty-four hours after delivery, in the opinion of this group. Nursing is more successful if it begins immediately, and mothers should continue to nurse as long as possible before switching to commercial formula. The committee also recommended that the breast-fed baby should be given vitamin and mineral supplements—particularly vitamin D, iron, and fluoride—and that the baby should not be fed solid foods until it is four to six months old. The digestive system of an infant is not ready to assimilate proteins found in foods other than breast milk or formula, nor are his kidneys strong enough to deal with the protein and the minerals of solid fare.

Breast milk has the additional virtue of containing only a small amount of salt, a fraction of that in cows' and goats' milk. A high sodium content in a child's diet may well predispose him to hypertension in adulthood or even earlier. (One alarming report revealed that more than 10 percent of children between the ages of ten and thirteen are hypertensive.)

Breast-fed babies regulate their own intake. When babies are fed from the bottle, it is the mother who determines when the baby has had enough. A baby who listens to his own internal hunger signals is less likely ever to be compliant when someone urges food upon him that he neither wants nor needs.

The Surgeon General himself, Dr. C. Everett Koop, has now declared mother's milk to be "not substitutable." It is the source of the most complete nutrition for babies, and it provides them with extra immunity from childhood illness. "People who say they can't afford the best for their children already have it," Dr. Koop points out.

(Nowadays, more and more women choose to—or must— combine motherhood with full-time employment outside the home. "There is a lack of passionate commitment to the pregnancy," Dr. T. Berry Brazelton, the eminent pediatrician, has observed of these working women. "They don't have the dreams and fears and fantasies normal to most expectant mothers. It's as if they are guarding themselves from the turmoil of attachment. As if they are grieving already for what might be lost.")

A measure of the state of its civilization is any society's attitude toward its handicapped and its dependents. It is a confession of the grossest neglect if a nation as much as admits that it cannot be burdened with the problem of every hapless child, whether it be assuaging hunger pangs, correcting dental problems or visual impairments, helping children to learn how to read, removing barriers to learning, or finding loving homes for the homeless. If we hope to distinguish ourselves as a truly civilized society, we could make no better start than by taking care of our children. Over the past quarter century, there has been a doubling of the number of children under seventeen years of age who have been limited by chronic health disabilities.

Until recent times, children did not exist as an entity in our society. They were regarded as miniature adults who mingled, competed, worked, and socialized with their elders. Only with the rise of the Industrial Revolution was the attitude toward them revised. The world was made aware—no more eloquently than through the novels of Charles Dickens—of the abuses heaped upon children working long hours in factories.

At last, youngsters were perceived as delicate and in need of nurturing. They *were* different from adults.

"Instead of fulfilling the three-score and ten as the allotted life of man," the American educator Horace Mann remarked, in 1842, "almost one-quarter part of the race perishes before attaining *one-seventieth* part of their natural term of existence. Before the age of five, up to one-third of all people born die."

Nearly 150 years later, the picture for children worldwide is still exceedingly grim. Of the 125 million children born every year in the 1980s, 17 million will be dead before their fifth birthday. Unless there is some civilized turnaround, conditions are likely to worsen for the world's poorest children. In this "silent emergency," 40,000 children quietly die of infection and malnutrition *every day,* 100 million quietly go to sleep hungry *every night,* and 10 million or more quietly become disabled in mind and body *every year.*

Our concern for our children seems to be selective.

"There is a madness in our society," say Milton Brutten, Sylvia O. Richardson, and Charles Mangel, authors of *Something's Wrong with My Child.* "It is a madness that allows us to acknowledge facts—and then to ignore them. It is the madness that allows us to boast of our dedication to children, and then, surely and competently, to destroy everyone who is not well and who has not been pulled out of the line of fire by his family. For this is the truth: in this country, few children get help when it is beyond the reach of their family. And that is our insanity."

The Joint Commission on Mental Health concluded that this country has no unified commitment to its children: "The claim that we are a child-centered society, that we look to our young as tomorrow's leaders, is a myth. This nation . . . gives no real help with child-rearing until a child is badly disturbed

143

and/or disruptive to the community. . . . Those who are the most helpless are the most neglected. . . . Most children, regardless of class or race, whether in the ghetto or suburbia, do not receive the needed support and assistance from our society. . . . Our lack of commitment is a national tragedy."

By the age of four, as many as 25 percent of the children in some poverty areas demonstrate crippled emotional development. Each year, increasing numbers are expelled from the community and confined in state hospitals so woefully understaffed that there are few, if any, professionals trained in child psychiatry and related disciplines. In any number of these massive warehouses for the mentally ill, it is not unusual to come upon children nine and ten years old who are locked up in a ward with eighty to ninety very sick adults.

"Far more valid research has been done (and more money spent) on raising pigs, chickens, corn, or cucumbers," writes Howard James, in *Children In Trouble*, "than on solving the problems of our troubled youth." (Contrast the uniquely healthful diet of animals at the zoo in Washington, D.C., with the devitalized, devitaminized, processed and additive-saturated "junk foods" in the diets of so many children that lead to problems.) Farmers have an effective lobby; most neglected children have had no one they can count on, no one who would speak for them, no one who would make demands for them. The agony of these children is met with a deaf ear by those who bear the responsibility for their survival.

At least two-thirds of the nation's children under fifteen years of age receive inadequate health care or none whatsoever. Yet at least one-third of all handicapping conditions could be prevented or corrected by comprehensive care of children until they are six years old. Close to half of all children are not adequately immunized, and half of all children under fifteen years of age have never been examined by a dentist.

Social commentator Vance Packard contends that ours is an "anti-child" culture. Putting our children first is not a common practice, he observes, and he quotes a sociologist, Amitai Etzione, as saying "roughly a third of United States schools actually inflict psychic harm on children."

"Child-rearing should be fun," as Dr. Lendon Smith has contended. "If it isn't fun, it won't work. Parents should be able to laugh more than cry, but what I see in many cases are vicious cycles of ill health that get started needlessly, largely through parents' ignorance of the preventive health approach. Mothers and fathers have been worrying about the wrong things and failing to do what they should about some terribly important symptoms and behaviors."

In the best of all worlds, parents would be blessed with that happy child who, as described by Dr. Smith, laughs and smiles more than he cries and frowns; rarely sneezes, snores, or coughs; does not bruise easily and cuts his teeth well; handles, with a minimum of stress, weather changes, going to school, learning new skills, meeting strangers, and other adaptations; likes many foods, even vegetables and salads; works up to his ability in school, easily learns to read, and usually is compliant and easygoing; is adroit and coordinated and neither thin nor fat; has few extremes of emotional response—he cries or laughs appropriately; does not prolong bed-rocking, thumb-sucking, or hair-twisting; is easily toilet-trained; enjoys pleasing others; is adept at entertaining himself; is fun to have around and can even remember birthdays. . . .

"Know you what it is to be a child?" the English poet Francis Thompson asked, summoning images obviously of a *healthy* child. "It is to be something very different from the man of today. It is to have a spirit yet streaming from the waters of baptism; it is to believe in love, to believe in loveliness, to believe in belief; it is to be so little that the elves can reach to whisper in your ear; it is to turn pumpkins into coaches and mice into horses, lowness into loftiness, and nothing into everything, for each child has its fairy godmother in its soul."

Another poet said simply, "Childhood is the kingdom where everything lives."

How wonderful if every child could dwell in that kingdom!

Chapter XII

Parenting and Finding the Progressive Pediatrician

UNFORTUNATELY, FOR REASONS complex and various, too many children do not inhabit that blessed kingdom the poet envisaged.

Nor do they vaguely fit that profile of the "happy child."

To be a child, for millions of the less fortunate, is to be wiggly, squirmy, fidgety, noisy, sobbing, headachy, fatigued, depressed, insomniac, cold, hungry.

There is everything to be said for good parenting, but after we have done all the right things—provided the optimal diet and boundless love and every opportunity imaginable—we can then only hope for the best. Sometimes there are other factors beyond our knowledge and control.

The mystery of human maturation is inexplicable. Extraordinary parents will have ordinary children, and brilliant children are born to unremarkable parents; genetic background is far, far from being fathomable or the whole story. The corporate chairman is dismayed that his son wants to become a ballet dancer, and the successful surgeon hangs his head in shame because Junior is playing in a rock band. But then there are the taxi driver whose son becomes an astrophysicist and the clerk in the hardware store whose daughter progresses to the presidency of an Ivy League college.

You as parents will spare yourselves much guilt and anguish if you can accept the diversities, limitations, temperaments, interests, and associations (within reasonable boundaries) of your children. And you'll be saving *them* immeasurable guilt and anguish. To some extent, we are the products of our environment. But an apparently similar environment can produce widely dissimilar individuals. One neglected truth is that not even identical twins raised together have identical environments.

"We know the negative things—abuse or neglect or acute deprivation—will scar or cripple forever a budding personality," the syndicated columnist Sydney Harris has written. "But there is no positive formula for success in childrearing. You do your best and you take your chances. Sometimes you win, sometimes you lose, sometimes you are dead before the votes are in."

Good parenting is a special—and onerous—challenge to the mother and the father of a learning disabled child. If parents are indeed crucial in the development of the healthily maturing child, they are that, and more, to the child with severe or even mild behavioral disorders. Only the home can provide the warm and sustained support this child needs. The burden of remedial measures lodges not in the classroom or in a therapist's office but in the home.

A realistic parent knows that not everything is "curable." Sometimes, the best thing we can do for a persistent and severe disability is to try to see to it that the child is not overpressed with a sense of being a "special problem" and that he does not become the obsession of the rest of the family. The learning disabled child, above all, needs firmness, consistency, and clarity

Routine to this child is what walls are to a house; it gives boundaries and dimensions to his life. A cool objectivity on your part as parent may be hard to achieve, but it can save both the day and your own sanity.

Even with effective treatment, academic work may for a while be difficult and erratic. But until your learning disabled child catches up, you as parents can do much to further his learning experiences. You can make of almost anything an activity in which he will learn. A trip to the supermarket, a Sunday afternoon drive, a sporting event, even mealtimes—all can be made educational. Anything is potentially an "exercise in practical life," in the words of Dr. Maria Montessori. Any aptitude your child picks up for doing this or that chore in the functioning of the household will counterbalance the sense of failure that his difficulties in school give him.

If your child is dyslexic, you will need a special amount of patience and forbearance. This is a disorder difficult to overcome. In my orthomolecular approach I am concerned first about altering in a beneficial way the brain chemistry of a dyslexic child. Once this has been accomplished, the child is susceptible to remedial tutoring, which enables him to catch up to his reading and writing grade levels. But until recent times, think how hopeless was the plight of the dyslexic. Because dyslexia is the most common of learning disorders, let me discourse briefly on the subject.

Specific dyslexia is a genetic, neurological dysfunction uncomplicated by other factors; it is not the result of brain damage, retardation, psychopathology, or poor teaching. On the continuum of childhood disabilities, a learning impairment is the least severe of disorders, frustrating as it is to the victim and to those around him. A child with dyslexia comes closest to being a normal or an average child. Because of his perceptual difficulties, he appears to be slow or not applying himself. The

149

longer his condition is undiagnosed, the more deep-seated becomes his aversion even to making an effort. He grows angry and hopeless about his accumulating failures. He feels incompetent and worthless and develops a sense of futility. Unless properly diagnosed at some time, he remains the helpless protagonist of a mystery that is never solved.

I know of the desperation secretly borne by a dyslexic woman until she was thirty-three years old. Hers is the now-familiar story of a child doing badly in school, being told to try harder, suffering the abuse of teachers and the taunts of her peers, and compensating by becoming the class clown. In high school she forsook academic courses for classes in sewing and cooking. Later, she had a series of jobs in which she did very well if written reports were not needed. She married, became a mother, and made grocery lists by copying words under pictures in newspaper advertisements. She followed the advice of a friend that she be tested, and it wasn't until then that she understood that her problem was her inability to visualize words or letters and keep them in her mind. She also learned that there were millions of other adults similarly handicapped. She formed a speakers' bureau to inform civic groups, teachers, and the media about dyslexia. Most people climb the educational mountain with the right kind of boots, she has observed, but the learning disabled do it in their bare feet.

Eileen Simpson overcame her dyslexia sufficiently to become a professional writer of genuine literary merit. She has likened the jamming, blocking, and confusion she suffered to a mechanical breakdown, to an out-of-order switchboard, or to two typewriter keys locking so that neither strikes the paper and prints. There was nothing wrong with her eyes; what was wrong was the message her eyes were transmitting to her brain. She was in the fourth grade and having grave difficulties with her schooling when Samuel P. Orton, an American neurologist and psychiatrist, postulated that children who were failing in school or who seemed to be dull might be the victims of a peculiar disorientation. In her case, Ms. Simpson was to discover poor spelling could not be completely eradicable. But it could be vastly improved through training in phonetics and the learning of basic rules like *i* before *e* except after *c*. (Interestingly, it was not in English but in Latin classes where she made notable progress toward literacy; Latin consonants and vowels and their combination represent predictable sounds, and the spelling of Latin words is not capricious and tricky, as English can be.)

You are well advised to be moderately strict in all areas affecting the safety and the well-being of your learning disabled child. But, please, be reasonably tolerant and flexible in matters relating to his personal taste preferences. His uniqueness must be respected. But his immaturity and gullibility may make him easy prey for others with delinquent proclivities. Here, your firm parental hand is needed, lest your child be drawn by peer pressure into antisocial—and possibly self-destructive—conduct.

Being infinitely patient with learning disabled children—so difficult at times, when they are ostensibly intelligent and so capable in some ways—should not preclude your punishing them. Punishment, when necessary, ought to be prompt and calm, so as not to add to the confusion of an already troubled child. You should make clear that it is the action, *not he,* that displeases you, and you should communicate this in a simple, nonpreachy, unsanctimonious way. Rewards are just as much in order as the occasional punishment. Here, timing is of the utmost importance. Deferred rewards mean nothing to the learning disabled child; his good behavior should be rewarded immediately. It is at home, more than anywhere else, that he will learn his value—that he is an essential member of the family, loved and lovable.

This is my checklist of dos and don'ts suggested for your orientation toward your learning disabled child:

- Expect, and brace yourself, for turmoil, and try to keep a lid on your emotions.

- Speak softly, even when enforcing discipline or dispensing punishment.

- Assign responsibility, but no more than one task at a time.

- Have a regular schedule for your child, and be sure to demonstrate anything new that you will expect of him.

- Try for a positive approach; find a way of avoiding all those phrases such as "stop that" or "mustn't do that."

- Consistency, consistency, consistency—you are your child's only anchor to windward.

- Give him his own space in the home and keep it sacrosanct for him. See that he plays with only one or two chums at a time; a group may be overwhelming.

- Refrain from mocking, pitying, mimicking, or overindulging him.

- Do not let him intimidate you.

- Be especially vigilant about medication: Keep it locked up, know the name and the proper dosage of any prescribed drugs, supervise their dispensation, and consult your doctor immediately about any misgivings you may have concerning a prescription.

Bad behavior, to reprise, is *not* synonymous with "bad child."

You as parents can be all-powerful in alleviating the distresses of your child. You, more than anyone else, can enable him to take his place alongside other children in the educational process. But you ought also to know your limitations, and I think the principal one is this: You should not try to assume the role of teacher in helping your child "catch up" academically. Even if you are a teacher by profession, there are too many emotions involved for you to be effective as the primary tutorial support of your child. However, it is wise to keep in close collaboration with his teachers and other professionals in helping him overcome his difficulties.

There is not too much you can expect regular schools to do for learning disabled children, other than what is already being done. We all know how overcrowded most classrooms are. Almost everywhere, local boards of education are hard-pressed to cope with the current costs of building and maintenance, salary demands of administrative staffs and teachers, and the threat of strikes by one faction or another.

With specialized help, your children can improve the perceptual skills that are deficient. Or there is the more general approach in which particular deficits are taken into account as they struggle with reading, writing, spelling, and arithmetic. The first approach assumes that children can be made educable by skilled intervention. The second is less ambitious and is based on the premise that school subjects should be taught in special ways that adjust to the inadequacies of learning disabled children.

153

Which approach is better? Making them less hard to teach, or teaching in a way that takes into account their being hard to teach? Or should both approaches be somehow combined, and, if so, in what proportions? The general thinking is that it depends: It depends upon a given child's age and the degree of the problem. The younger the child, presumably the better will be the response to the training of perceptual skills. For older children, it is better to be realistic and teach them to read, spell, calculate, and write in ways tailored to their needs.

The younger a learning disabled child is diagnosed, the greater is the hope that he will achieve his full potential academically. But recognizing realistic teaching dilemmas, I must say I find both of these approaches less than satisfactory. I do not believe there should be any compromises in our effort at least to educate all children to the limit of their capabilities. To make this goal realizable, we must first straighten out the twisted wires and disconnected synapses in the children's learning apparatus. Then we should train them in the specific skills that have been lagging and let each child proceed without any preconceived expectations of how high he can soar.

You should prepare yourself for one perverse turn in your child's otherwise steady progression out of his learning difficulties. As he catches his first full gaze at the light at the end of the tunnel, he may retreat into the darkness. This is his unconscious mind momentarily taking over and telling him not to let go of his handicap. "There are advantages in being 'different,'" a little voice assures him. "Think of all the special attention you get. Some people may make fun of you, but think how much more Mommy and Daddy fuss over you than they do over little brother or big sister. A lot of things will change if you become just like everybody else. . . ." The best way of heading off this regression is for you to create a home environment that does not pamper your child or make permissible conduct he knows is undesirable. Remind him what a relief it will be to him in particular not to be burdened with a lot of "baggage" that keeps him crawling instead of running.

There is no such thing as too much love, banal as that sounds. Along with the discipline, bushels of love and kisses are most appropriate, nearly indispensable, for your disabled child. Child-training is largely knowing which end of your child to pat—and when. Discipline applied with love usually works; applied with anger and rage, it rarely works, and only fills a child with dark thoughts of revenge.

"You know more than you think you do," as Dr. Benjamin Spock advised generations of parents in *Baby and Child Care*. "Love and enjoy your children for what they are, for what they look like, for what they do, and forget about the qualities they don't have. . . . The children who are appreciated for what they are, even if they are homely or clumsy or slow, will grow up with confidence in themselves—happy. They will have a spirit that will make the best of all the capabilities they have. . . . They will make light of any handicaps. But the children who have never been quite accepted by their parents, who have always felt they were not quite right, will grow up lacking confidence. . . . If they start life with a handicap, physical or mental, it will be multiplied tenfold by the time they are grown-up."

How wisely Dr. Spock speaks to the parents of a learning disabled child, as well as to all other parents!

In the sequence of events, before good parenting comes the search for an enlightened pediatrician.

Most first-time parents tend to find a pediatrician either through the obstetrician or the recommendation of close friends or the chief pediatric resident at a medical center. Residents of large cities have the luxury of choosing a doctor whose office is convenient in location, however irrelevant the factor of geography should be.

It is important to know a doctor's hospital affiliation. Should the infant or small child be taken seriously ill, he will require an institution with superior facilities. Teaching hospitals—those connected with medical schools—are highly recommended. A pediatrician on the attending staff is also likely to play some teaching role at the school.

Pediatricians are the only doctors who are "looked over" by the parents of their prospective patient before the patient is even born. This occurs at the pediatrician interview, which has become as routine among parents-to-be as picking out the carriage, crib, and layette and deciding that if it is a boy it will be Jesse or if it is a girl it will be Jessica. This interview is usually free of charge (it may be the only such service within the entire medical continuum from birth to death to have this distinction!), and you may find yourself interviewing more than one doctor before you come upon the ideal one.

Typically, an expectant mother in her seventh or eighth month of pregnancy will call for an appointment those pediatricians who have been recommended by one source or another. Her visit is the occasion for learning from the doctor his methodology and his underlying convictions about child raising. It is not enough for her to know whether she can call him at home in an emergency or whether he will make house calls. There may be any number of other questions she would like to ask him. Does he encourage the father to assume a strong parenting role? Does he have a deep understanding of, and commitment to, nutrition? Is he informed about allergies, which, as we have noted, are increasingly prevalent among children today? Is he medication-oriented or does he place more reliance on the preventive medicine of proper dietary habits and vitamin supplementation? Does he believe in natural foods and deplore the eating habits most children soon fall into?

Advising again as a nutrition-biased psychiatrist, I would suggest you sound out the doctor about his views on weight gains. Too many pediatricians are obsessed with having babies gain weight by whatever means, and weight gain through the consumption of sugar and starchy foods does not produce a healthy child. In the interest of weight gains, sugar water and sugar-loaded formulas are given in some hospital nurseries! A child can attain normal growth without ever consuming refined sugar.

Many infants who are not breast-fed and are put on solids too early soon learn that they must stuff themselves to please Mommy. In the minds of young children, eating heartily soon becomes identified with winning both love and approval. They are torn between trying to please and placate this big, commanding figure and the wish to refuse food because they are not hungry. Eating beyond need or satiety at an early age can be the genesis of an obesity problem that will last a lifetime. Babies who have been breast-fed for at least six months rarely become overweight as child or adult. Today, we are seeing far more pre-adolescent children who are dangerously overweight than ever before, and we can assume that their poor eating habits began in infancy. Overeating is a negation of good nutrition.

A good pediatrician knows the advantages of the vitamin and other nutrient supplements administered to children. He knows that, with these nutritional boosters, babies—and growing children—have fewer general health complaints. But most pediatricians who do recommend the supplements would be reluctant to endorse any treatment involving dosages far in excess of the Recommended Daily Allowances. Still, there are pediatricians aplenty who recognize a developing learning disability when they see it, and more and more of them are apprised of the orthomolecular approach and are sympathetic to it.

The pediatrician who is being interviewed may show signs of irritation if the probing is extended and demanding. So be it. It is vital that the parents make the best possible choice. This will be one of the longest continuing relationships that a mother will have with any doctor. She must have confidence in his expertise.

A mother will learn to listen with her "third ear." It is *how* the prospective baby doctor answers the questions as well as *what* he says. She will gather considerable data from his expression and his general attitude. Curt yes-and-no responses should rule him out immediately. If he is distracted or overly busy on the telephone with extraneous matters, such as taking a call from his broker or discussing social engagements, or if he is riffling through his mail, he surely will be found wanting in attentiveness when he is really needed.

A look around the offices and waiting room will be informative. Does he put out jars of candies or lollipops? If he does, he may be kindly but hardly an advanced or nutrition-wise pediatrician.

The ultimate in pediatric sensitivity is the doctor who can distinguish among the different cries of infants, much in the way that ornithologists will identify birds by their notes. Babies cry for all the normal reasons, of course. But there are different cries signifying neurological disorders, metabolic problems, anatomical irregularities, various syndromes, or chromosomal abnormalities. Even mental retardation can be detected in the way a baby cries.

The parents-to-be will want to know who will substitute for the doctor when he is not available. Who "sits in" for him when he takes ill, goes on holiday, or attends medical meetings and conferences out of town? Some pediatricians have the same telephone number at home as at the office and theoretically can be contacted at any time of the day or night. Others can be reached through an answering service, but an answering service is at best less than satisfactory. Quite commonly, when the pediatrician is not available, his nurse will come on the phone. Some mothers are frustrated talking to the nurse instead of to the doctor, but it is only fair to point out that an experienced nurse is adept in counseling on many routine matters, and often she can be more patient because she is less harassed than the doctor.

Everyone should be forthright about the question of fees. Ask the pediatrician directly how much he charges. Find out how often he will want to see your baby. During that crucial first year, there should be enough visits so that the doctor can monitor social, motor, and intellectual development.

The pediatrician is rarely at the hospital when the mother delivers (the baby is examined instantly by an attending physician), but he certainly should see the newborn within twenty-four hours. In that initial visit, when he makes the acquaintance of the infant, he can instruct first-time mothers on how to breast-feed.

The office hours of most pediatricians may seem to be honored more in the "breach." Teaching responsibilities and attending to newborns can take a doctor out of the office at all hours of the day. Some pediatricians, particularly in the larger cities, will usually try to set aside an hour or two each day as their "call-in" time. This gives them the opportunity to reply to routine, nonemergency questions: "How do I get my child to eat oatmeal?"; "Why does my three-year-old have a fixation on vacuum cleaners?"; "Should my four-year-old be allowed to look at the evening news on television?"

The subject of house calls has in recent years become the stuff of satire. Pediatricians will contend, perhaps self-servingly, that they prefer to see sick children in their offices, where more effective treatment is available. This is little comfort to the worried parent who believes the child should not be taken out of doors when he has a fever or the weather is inclement. Most doctors, I feel confident, will make a house call if it really is an emergency or if the parent, too, is ill and cannot take the child to the doctor's office.

Some really fine pediatricians become almost famous and inspire such rapturous descriptions as: "knows how to make parents laugh about their own foibles"; "doesn't talk down to the parents"; "kisses, cuddles, and talks to the children"; "knows a lot of things like pediatric pulmonology and ne-phrology"; "a fantastic diagnostician"; "like an old country doctor, sweet and unpretentious"; "relaxed and easygoing, never gets excited"; "takes a stand and is assertive"; "very tol-erant and doesn't underestimate what mothers feel."

Yes, you are certainly within your rights to change doctors if you are not completely happy with the one you choose. There can be any number of reasons for dissatisfaction, you and your child and the doctor all being human, and family and doctor may not necessarily be "meant" for each other. If your doctor never remembers your child's name or if he gives misinfor-mation about tests or if he is too often brusque and abrupt because he habitually overbooks his day, well . . .

Parents have understandable fears and anxieties about changing doctors. Some are worried that important records will not travel from one pediatrician to the next. This is a needless concern; professional courtesy requires that all records be transferred promptly. In changing doctors, nothing more is required than the common consideration of calling the un-satisfactory doctor and saying, simply, "We feel we would like to try another pediatrician."

Parenting and Finding the Progressive Pediatrician

The element of luck cannot be discounted in any area of life, including the search for the best pediatrician available. But it seems to me that a certain amount of intuition and some preconceived and precise guidelines should put the new parents or the parents-to-be on the road to the choice of an excellent doctor.

The incidence of learning disorders—ranging from mild to severe—is increasing, and parents are becoming more sophisticated on these matters. Fewer and fewer parents will be pacified with the nimble evasions of a pediatrician when they suspect a real problem is developing. They will begin to have their doubts about a doctor who dispenses such familiar bromides as "boys are slower than girls," "boys will be boys," "calm down, he'll be just fine," "many healthy children do not speak until they are four years old," or "so your baby rolls across the rug instead of creeping on hands and knees, there is nothing to worry about." If a condition varies much from what is considered to be the norm, any conscientious parent will want to explore the possibilities of the cause and not settle for a "pacifier."

Fortunately, more and more pediatricians are becoming alert to the symptoms of emotional, learning, and developmental disorders. In the best sense, they are protecting their young patients from those parents who may be only too prone to put on blinders to keep themselves from seeing what they do not wish to see. An increasing number of primary doctors recognize that a disturbed sleep pattern, nonstop hustle and bustle, attention deficit, or chronic unruliness indeed reflect underlying problems that should be dealt with immediately. These doctors are not hesitating to advise a parent to take a child for diagnostic evaluation. They are proving a valuable adjunct to the total care of the child. They counsel the parents sympathetically on how—as a caring guardian—to seek the necessary treatment.

Chapter XIII

Toward a Hopeful, Healthful Future

IDEALLY, MEDICINE SHOULD be a pragmatic profession. It should do its energetic best to cure—or at least to relieve—patients of their hurts or illnesses. From the scientific point of view it is valuable to know why something works and why something else does not work. Medical tradition at its most exemplary is characterized by the phrase *nil nisi bono*—nothing unless good.

The annals of medicine are replete with rejections of new approaches for no other reason than that the new approaches are incongruous with traditional modes of medical thinking and practice. If psychiatry—especially as it addresses the problems of disordered children—is to remain within the family of medicine, it must take a new direction; it will need to think and to act more like an exponent of biological medicine.

It may seem paradoxical that it is the public itself, rather than the medical profession, that must lead the way to protecting the common health. It was the public, acting through the Popular Health Movement and related groups in the last century, that led to improved sanitation and living standards and general education on matters of health and personal hygiene. It was the public, in the early 1900s, that fought the unconscionable proliferation of fraudulent patent medicines and the unsanitary practices of the food industry; this confrontation led directly to the passage of the landmark Food and Drug Act of 1906. More recently, it was the public—young people in particular—that sparked the agitation for a cleaner environment, which culminated in Earth Day 1970; Earth Day, in turn, was the precursor for such environmental regulations as the Toxic Substances Control Act of 1976.

Within the United States there is an active movement, as we all know, in the direction of preventive medicine. People are beginning to see the folly of waiting for an illness to develop, only to be treated with drugs that suppress symptoms but do little to eradicate the illness. They are aware that medicine is an industry that costs Americans billions of dollars a year. They are no longer content to be merely patients; they are looking for medical care that can help them *avoid* illness.

The wave of the future will certainly be movements like Robert Rodale's People's Medical Society. He is suggesting nothing less than that the massive medical/health establishment in the United States be turned around truly to benefit the private citizen. Health care must become less expensive; prevention of illness must be a primary goal rather than the ugly stepsister of medicine.

Somewhat along the same lines, Derek C. Bok, the president of Harvard University, is calling for changes in training of American physicians at every stage. Specifically, he has asked that more attention be given to such neglected areas of knowledge as the ethics of medicine, patient psychology, and methods of prevention.

Congruous with what Mr. Bok is saying, medicine is being held far more accountable today than it was fifteen or twenty years ago. With the growing distrust of *all* authority, much of the public is becoming disenchanted with medicine as a profession that is neither benevolent nor altruistic. That cynicism will continue to extend to psychiatry, as one branch of medicine, if it fails to explore innovative and inexpensive treatments that might prove widely effective.

The capacity to eliminate disease does not equal the capacity to create health. The waiting rooms of every general practitioner are filled with people who have no specific disease. But neither are they healthy. They yearn to feel better and to live a more vigorous and joyous life. Lamentably, too many GPs are still in the business of sickness care, not of health care. Insurance companies still pay freely for prescribed drugs and for extended treatment of disease, but they do not reimburse the insured for a visit to the doctor for counsel on good nutrition and on the techniques for preventing illness.

Patients in the future will be increasingly well informed on medical matters. They will choose and use their doctors more wisely; they will no longer be satisfied with a once-over-lightly annual physical "checkup" and shuffled along their way with some all-service injunction, such as "You could do with a vacation" or "Better cut down on your weight" (or smoking or drinking). They will not be ushered out with a prescription for a tranquilizer or an anxiolytic drug. They will be demanding specific counsel on how to make the best long-range investment in their health. They will ask for individualized vitamin profiles to fit their needs. They will want to know how they *naturally* can avoid the immunosuppressive action of stresses and depressions, and they will not be put off with the simplistic explanation that "Everybody has them from time to time" or "You'll just have to learn to live with them, that's life."

Under good doctoring in the years to come, patients with

even severe maladies will fare as well by being treated at home as in a modern hospital equipped with all the latest gadgetry; the familiarity and warmth of home counterbalance the advantages of technology in a strange and forbidding atmosphere. Patients will be attended by doctors who have recovered the lost art of listening and who will know that the human spirit is as much to be ministered to as the body. "I had a fast-growing conviction," recalled Norman Cousins in *Anatomy of an Illness,* "that a hospital is no place for a person who is seriously ill."

Leaving emotional sustenance aside, Mr. Cousins found that the hospital failed abyssmally in the area of nutrition. He complained of poorly balanced meals, of highly processed, additive-heavy foods, overcooked vegetables, and doughy white bread. Subscribing to "the wisdom of the body," he took the matter of nutrition into his own hands and prescribed for himself 25 grams of vitamin C every day. These megadosages began to cut heavily into whatever poison had been attacking his connective tissue; his fever receded; his pulse stopped racing; and in what he regarded as nothing short of "a miracle" he was soon back at his editorial duties.

I feel sure that Mr. Cousins would join me in sincere cheers for C. B. Pennington, a Louisiana oil baron. In the largest gift ever bestowed upon a university ($125 million), Mr. Pennington has stipulated that the money be used to build "the country's biggest and best nutrition and preventive medicine center" and that it should be built near the university campus at Baton Rouge. He said that he wanted to "put all my eggs in one basket" and build a facility that would win recognition throughout the world. Few persons in history have an opportunity to change human events for the better for millions, and fewer still avail themselves of the opportunity.

Increasingly, the mentally ill in our country are homeless

people. In our large cities, in particular, they are being treated as common criminals or they are being neglected completely. At best, they have the worst of two worlds. Countless thousands of them are needlessly confined to institutions; thousands of others are simply abandoned. In many places, it is worse than the Middle Ages, when at least some communities cared for their mentally ill and did not ostracize or banish them. The same, to a lesser degree, applies to learning disabled children when they are improperly diagnosed or treated with contempt by peers and teachers.

So much human potential can be realized and so much suffering alleviated when proper diagnosis and help are available early.

The various biological discoveries have greatly increased man's life expectancy. But at one end of the life spectrum are the children who face consignment to hopeless abandonment. These seriously disordered children—be they schizophrenic; autistic; Down's syndrome; mentally retarded, brain-injured, or cerebral-palsied—are incapable of protesting their fate. Parents are urged to "put them away," and no expert testimony is necessary to insure the incarceration of mere youngsters. In most states, there is not even the requirement—as there is for the institutionalization of a psychotic adult—that at least two physicians certify that confinement is necessary.

Still, federal law does specify that all handicapped children must be given classroom education. A mixed blessing. There are teachers and parents alike who don't want "mainstreaming." At the very least, this legislation throws the spotlight on something still generally missing. We lack an adequate core of scientific investigators with solid grounding in research techniques for teaching the learning disabled.

There are hopeful signs of progress. We do have nongraded schools that emphasize organization and structure in the teaching of language skills. The Kingsbury Lab School, in our nation's capital, strives to help children learn to "differentiate" and to "integrate" words, to denote the ability to distinguish one thing from another and then to file the information in appropriate mental slots—and to help the children develop knowledge and sequence. The school's foremost aim is to "give our students the social tools that will allow them to utilize their learning effectively, to function in life independently and as useful members of society."

Still, I think we lag behind some of the other developed countries. I have been impressed by the superior learning opportunities for handicapped children in some European schools. In the Netherlands, specialized schooling is completely free, and I have asked how this was possible. "Oh, it is written into the national constitution," I was informed. "Every child should be educated to the limit of his ability. We in special education tell the government what we plan for these youngsters, and they must by law give it to us."

The United States has an average of one psychologist for every three elementary schools. Millions of school-age children are desperately in need of assistance, but this is the Era of Cutting Corners. When the child is undernourished, or comes to school in shabby clothing that makes him the butt of jokes, or is having inherent difficulties in learning to read, we have problems beyond the scope of the best and the most conscientious classroom teachers.

We have principals who won't allow classes for retarded children in their schools. We have teachers who belittle or disparage the learning disabled in front of other students. Our educators must accept children who have impairments handicapping their progress with the three Rs, and, even more to the point, they must develop an understanding that will empower them to point the way toward removing these impairments. We in this land known as the world's first example of equal educational opportunity have among us tens of millions of complete illiterates and an additional eight million who are classified as functional illiterates; most of these are like strangers in their own land, unable to read street signs or transportation routes or to read or write well enough to complete an employment application.

All children can learn. When they do not learn, something is interfering with the natural learning process. We hear considerable discussion these days about the woeful decline in the state of education. But too little is being said about the plight of the multitudes of children who are not even being helped to become educable. The parents of a handicapped child must demand that he, too, will have an equal opportunity to learn. Not the opportunity to learn *if* he can read without major assistance, not the opportunity to learn *if* he is physically unimpaired but simply the opportunity to learn—whoever he is.

Under federal direction, we inquire into the income status of families in order to determine who is eligible for subsidies in the school cafeterias. The same determination may extend to eligibility for remedial programs, and thus exclude many children from less impecunious homes whose learning problems are real and require help. This is unfair. No children should be barred from available help with their impediments to learning because their families are not at the bottom of the economic scale.

More than a decade ago, the pediatrician Virginia Apgar was recommending that there be special diagnostic centers in the medical departments of the principal universities and a nationwide network of regional diagnostic centers. These centers would test children for emotional and learning disorders. As time went by, more and more hyperactive children would be seen by medical students, interns, and residents. The desirable consequence of this development would be that fewer and fewer top neurologists and pediatricians would still be clinging to the belief that medical examinations, EEGs, and investigation into sensory defects were irrelevant in evaluating hyperactivity.

Realistically, what parents can do for their learning disabled child or children depends upon their understanding—and perseverance—in seeking professional assistance. Leaving a hyperactive child in the hands of the family physician means that he will be treated within the boundaries of that physician's possibly limited expertise. The most that can be expected of the general practitioner is guidance to a special consultant. Only the specialist will be enabled to search for the physiological causes underlying a youngster's behavioral symptoms—causes that may be organic, metabolic, or toxic.

There are things we can do for our children besides loving them and hoping for the best. We can at the very least try to make them healthier young beings, and the primary way of doing this is seeing to it that their diet consists of the very finest of foods. We should also be as steadfast in seeing to it that they get help for any learning or behavioral disorders as we are in taking them to the doctor when anything is amiss with their physical health.

Orthomolecular therapy belongs to the future. The persuasion of efficacy is on its side. Thousands upon thousands of improved and recovered children (and adults) are living testimony for a treatment that has succeeded after so many other techniques have failed.

"If all physicians who refer patients to me were themselves to practice orthomolecular psychiatry, that is, the proper incorporation of nutritional therapy and practice into psychiatric treatment," the Canadian orthomolecular pioneer Dr. Abram

Hoffer has said to me, "I would immediately lose 85 percent of my practice."

I am continually being asked why orthomolecular medicine is not being practiced more widely. My first response is that "it *is* being practiced widely—and its acceptance is constantly spreading. Because it is so effective, it cannot be suppressed or derailed by antagonistic forces. Orthomolecular treatment centers are flourishing not only in this country but in Canada, Germany, France, Switzerland, and Australia as well."

I do concede that our approach remains controversial. Critics of orthomolecular medicine will say that what is needed is another carefully controlled double-blind study and long-term follow-ups before this therapy can earn the "Seal of Approval." ("Double-blind" describes the process of proving out medical theories by having the trials or testings of a new therapy or remedy run whenever possible in such a way that the judging clinician and the patient are unaware when the patient is taking medication or following a prescribed route toward the amelioration of symptoms or maladies.) To which we practitioners reply, "There already have been numerous double-blind studies. There have been countless papers and pamphlets—even books—proclaiming the successful results of these studies." *Another* double-blind study conservatively would require twelve more years. During this time an estimated 300,000 young people would have become intractably ill; hundreds of thousands of others would have developed learning disabilities in varying degrees. That seems such a high price to pay to meet some quite arbitrary recommendation.

"Nothing will ever be attempted if all possible objections must first be overcome," as Dr. Samuel Johnson observed.

Indeed. Many empirical forms of medical treatment are widely adopted without incontrovertible evidence of their efficacy. The use of antibiotic prophylaxis to treat chronic lung disease, anticoagulants to prevent strokes, and steroids for chronic liver diseases are three examples. "Claims of effectiveness of the treatment should be accepted if a substantial amount of well-documented favorable evidence is presented," to quote the National Academy of Sciences, "even though there may also be a weighty body of inconclusive or negative evidence."

"When two physiologists or two doctors quarrel, each to maintain his own ideas or theories, in the midst of their contradictory arguments, only one thing is absolutely certain: that both theories are insufficient and neither of them corresponds to the truth," wrote French physiologist Claude Bernard, in 1865. "We really know very little and we are fallible when facing the immense difficulties presented by investigation of natural phenomena. The best thing, then, for us to do is to unite our efforts instead of dividing them and nullifying them by personal disputes. In a word, the man of science wishing to find the truth must keep his mind free and calm and if it be possible never have his eye bedewed, as Bacon says, 'by human passion.'"

We practitioners of orthomolecular medicine must resist becoming defensive. "If it's so damned good," we are taunted, "why isn't everybody using it?" It would be so tempting to rejoin, "The reason everyone isn't using it is precisely because it *is* almost too 'damned good' to be believed."

I think it becomes us more to admit that we do not have all the answers to all the enigmas in medicine. But we can certainly take pride in the recognition our fledgling therapy has gained in the three decades in which it has been practiced. *And this recognition is based upon results.*

I also believe that basic research into the biochemical nature of learning disabilities of children will continue. It will lead to the establishment of scientific criteria for recognizing youngsters whose unique biochemical privations make them susceptible to improvement through orthomolecular therapy.

I believe very strongly that the rapid growth of interest in the nutritional approach to treatment is a unique episode in medical history. With the passing of the years, orthomolecular treatment has not remained a static, fixed discipline bound by dogma and orthodoxy. Nor has it abandoned its awareness that truth is only relative and that it must yield to contradiction if and when it is challenged by concrete, opposing data. Because it is flexible and evolving, orthomolecular medicine has found application in a broad variety of nervous and emotional symptoms and medical conditions.

I believe, too, that this is only a beginning. Future practitioners will carry orthomolecular medicine into areas none of us at this time can even envision.

Appendix A:

Questionnaire

I ASK PARENTS TO complete the following form before bringing in their learning disabled child for consultation. The subjects concern certain aberrant behavior and development that may have occurred in the years from birth to age five. The responses to the questionnaire enable me to formulate a profile, however inexact, of the child and the nature of his difficulties.

The questionnaire was originally developed by Bernard Rimland, Ph.D., Director, Institute for Child Behavior Research, 4182 Adams Avenue, San Diego, CA 92116.

Name of child _____

Birthdate _____

Person completing this form: _____

Street address: _____

City: _____

Zip _____

Dr. Cott's Help for Your Learning Disabled Child

Relationship to child:

Mother _____

Father _____ Other _____

Father's occupation _____

Mother's occupation (present) _____

  (Before marriage) _____

Has this child been diagnosed before?

  If so, what was diagnosis: _____

    Diagnosed by: _____

    Where? _____

USE AN "X" TO MARK ONE ANSWER FOR EACH QUESTION.

1. Present age of child:
   - _____ 1 Under 3 years old
   - _____ 2 Between 3 and 4 years old
   - _____ 3 Between 4 and 5 years old
   - _____ 4 Between 5 and 6 years old
   - _____ 5 Over 6 years old (Age: __ years)

2. Indicate child's sex:
   - _____ 1 Boy
   - _____ 2 Girl

3. Child's birth order and number of mother's other children:
   - _____ 1 Child is an only child
   - _____ 2 Child is first born of __ children
   - _____ 3 Child is last born of __ children
   - _____ 4 Child is middle born; __ children are older and __ are younger than this child
   - _____ 5 Foster child, or don't know

4. Were pregnancy and delivery normal?
   _____ 1 Pregnancy and delivery both normal
   _____ 2 Problems during both pregnancy and delivery
   _____ 3 Pregnancy troubled, routine delivery
   _____ 4 Pregnancy untroubled; problems during delivery
   _____ 5 Don't know

5. Was the birth premature (birth weight under 5 lbs)?
   _____ 1 Yes (about __ weeks early; __ lbs)
   _____ 2 No
   _____ 3 Don't know

6. Was the child given oxygen *in the first week?*
   _____ 1 Yes
   _____ 2 No
   _____ 3 Don't know

7. Appearance of child during first few weeks after birth:
   _____ 1 Pale, delicate looking
   _____ 2 Unusually healthy looking
   _____ 3 Average, don't know, or other

8. Unusual conditions of birth and infancy (check only one number in left-hand column):
   _____ 1 Unusual conditions (indicate which: blindness __, cerebral palsy __, birth injury __, seizures __, blue baby __, very high fever __, jaundice __, other _____)
   _____ 2 Twin birth (identical __, fraternal __)
   _____ 3 Both 1 and 2
   _____ 4 Normal, or don't know

177

9. Concerning baby's health in first 3 months:
     _____ 1 Excellent health, no problems
     _____ 2 Respiration (frequent infections ___,
             other _____)
     _____ 3 Skin (rashes ___, infection ___, allergy ___,
             other _____)
     _____ 4 Feeding (learning to suck ___, colic ___,
             vomiting ___, other _____)
     _____ 5 Elimination (diarrhea ___, constipation ___,
             other _____)
     _____ 6 Several of above (indicate which: 2 ___, 3 ___,
             4 ___, 5 ___, 6 ___)

10. Has the child been given an electroencephalogram (EEG)?
     _____ 1 Yes, it was considered normal
     _____ 2 Yes, it was considered borderline
     _____ 3 Yes, it was considered abnormal
     _____ 4 No, or don't know, or don't know
             results

11. In the first year, did the child react to bright lights, bright
    colors, unusual sounds, etc.?
     _____ 1 Unusually strong reaction (pleasure ___,
             dislike ___)
     _____ 2 Unusually unresponsive
     _____ 3 Average, or don't know

12. Did the child behave normally for a time before his abnormal behavior began?

　　—— 1 Never was a period of normal behavior
　　—— 2 Normal during first 6 months
　　—— 3 Normal during first year
　　—— 4 Normal during first 1½ years
　　—— 5 Normal during first 2 years
　　—— 6 Normal during first 3 years
　　—— 7 Normal during first 4–5 years

13. (Age 4–8 months) Did the child reach out or prepare to be picked up when mother approached him?

　　—— 1 Yes, or I believe so
　　—— 2 No, I don't think he did
　　—— 3 No, definitely not
　　—— 4 Don't know

14. Did the child rock in his crib as a baby?

　　—— 1 Yes, quite a lot
　　—— 2 Yes, sometimes
　　—— 3 No, or very little
　　—— 4 Don't know

15. At what age did the child learn to walk alone?

　　—— 1　8–12 months
　　—— 2 13–15 months
　　—— 3 16–18 months
　　—— 4 19–24 months
　　—— 5 25–36 months
　　—— 6 37 months or later, or does not walk
　　　　　alone

16. Which describes the change from crawling to walking?
    _____ 1 Normal change from crawling to walking
    _____ 2 Little or no crawling, gradual start of walking
    _____ 3 Little or no crawling, sudden start of walking
    _____ 4 Prolonged crawling, sudden start of walking
    _____ 5 Prolonged crawling, gradual start of walking
    _____ 6 Other, or don't know

17. During the child's first year, did it seem to be unusually intelligent?
    _____ 1 Suspected high intelligence
    _____ 2 Suspected average intelligence
    _____ 3 Child looked somewhat dull

18. During the child's first 2 years, did it like to be held?
    _____ 1 Liked being picked up; enjoyed being held
    _____ 2 Limp and passive on being held
    _____ 3 You could pick child up and hold it only when and how it preferred
    _____ 4 Notably stiff and awkward to hold
    _____ 5 Don't know

19. Before age 3, did the child ever imitate another person?
    ____ 1 Yes, waved bye-bye
    ____ 2 Yes, played pat-a-cake
    ____ 3 Yes, other (_____)
    ____ 4 Two or more of above (which? 1 __, 2 __,
          3 _)
    ____ 5 No, or not sure

20. Before age 3, did the child have an unusually good memory?
    ____ 1 Remarkable memory for songs,
          rhymes, TV commercials, etc., in
          words
    ____ 2 Remarkable memory for songs, music
          (humming only)
    ____ 3 Remarkable memory for names, places,
          routes, etc.
    ____ 4 No evidence for remarkable memory
    ____ 5 Apparently rather poor memory
    ____ 6 Both 1 and 3
    ____ 7 Both 2 and 3

21. Did you ever suspect the child was very nearly deaf?
    ____ 1 Yes
    ____ 2 No

22. (Age 2–4) Is child "deaf" to some sounds but hears others?
    ____ 1 Yes, can be "deaf" to loud sounds, but
          hears low ones
    ____ 2 No, this is not true of him

23. (Age 2–4) Does child hold his hands in strange postures?
_____ 1 Yes, sometimes or often
_____ 2 No

24. (Age 2–4) Does child engage in rhythmic or rocking activity for very long periods of time (like on rocking-horse or chair, jump-chair, swing, etc.)?
_____ 1 Yes, this is typical
_____ 2 Seldom does this
_____ 3 Not true of him

25. (Age 2–4) Does the child ever "look through" or "walk through" people, as though they weren't there?
_____ 1 Yes, often
_____ 2 Yes, I think so
_____ 3 No, doesn't do this

26. (Age 2–5) Does child have any unusual cravings for things to eat or chew on?
_____ 1 Yes, salt or salty foods
_____ 2 Yes, often chews metal objects
_____ 3 Yes, other (_____)
_____ 4 Yes, more than 2 above (which? ____)
_____ 5 No, or not sure

27. (Age 2–4) Does the child have certain eating oddities such as refusing to drink from a transparent container, eating only hot (or cold) food, eating only one or two foods, etc.?
_____ 1 Yes, definitely
_____ 2 No, or not to any marked degree
_____ 3 Don't know

28. Would you describe your child around age 3 or 4 as often seeming "in a shell," or so distant and "lost in thought" that you couldn't reach him?
    _____ 1 Yes, this is a very accurate description
    _____ 2 Once in a while might possibly be like that
    _____ 3 Not an accurate description

29. (Age 2–5) Is the child cuddly?
    _____ 1 Definitely, likes to cling to adults
    _____ 2 Above average (likes to be held)
    _____ 3 No, rather stiff and awkward to hold
    _____ 4 Don't know

30. (Age 3–5) Does the child deliberately hit his own head?
    _____ 1 Never, or rarely
    _____ 2 Yes, usually by slapping it with his hand
    _____ 3 Yes, usually by banging it against someone else's legs or head
    _____ 4 Yes, usually by hitting walls, floor, furniture, etc.
    _____ 5 Several of above (which? 2 ___, 3 ___, 4 ___)

31. (Age 3–5) How well physically coordinated is the child (running, walking, balancing, climbing)?
    _____ 1 Unusually graceful
    _____ 2 About average
    _____ 3 Somewhat below average, or poor

32. (Age 3–5) Does the child sometimes whirl like a top?
    _____ 1 Yes, does this often
    _____ 2 Yes, sometimes
    _____ 3 Yes, if you start him out
    _____ 4 No, he shows no tendency to whirl

33. (Age 3–5) How skillful is the child in doing fine work with his fingers or playing with small objects?
    _____ 1 Exceptionally skillful
    _____ 2 Average for age
    _____ 3 A little awkward, or very awkward
    _____ 4 Don't know

34. (Age 3–5) Does the child like to spin things like jar lids, coins, or coasters?
    _____ 1 Yes, often and for rather long periods
    _____ 2 Very seldom, or never

35. (Age 3–5) Does child show an *unusual* degree of skill (much better than normal child his age) at any of following:
    _____ 1 Assembling jigsaw or similar puzzles
    _____ 2 Arithmetic computation
    _____ 3 Can tell day of week a certain date will fall on
    _____ 4 Perfect musical pitch
    _____ 5 Throwing and/or catching a ball
    _____ 6 Other (_____)
    _____ 7 More than one of above (which? _____)
    _____ 8 No unusual skill, or not sure

36. (Age 3–5) Does the child sometimes jump up and down gleefully when pleased?

    ____ 1 Yes, this is typical

    ____ 2 No, or rarely

37. (Age 3–5) Does child sometimes line things up in precise, evenly spaced rows and insist they not be disturbed?

    ____ 1 No

    ____ 2 Yes

    ____ 3 Not sure

38. (Age 3–5) Does the child refuse to use its hands for an extended period of time?

    ____ 1 Yes

    ____ 2 No

39. Was there a time before age 5 when the child *strongly* insisted on listening to music on records?

    ____ 1 Yes, insisted on only certain records

    ____ 2 Yes, but almost any record would do

    ____ 3 Liked to listen, but didn't *demand* to

    ____ 4 No special interest in records

40. (Age 3–5) How interested is the child in mechanical objects such as the stove or vacuum cleaner?

    ____ 1 Little or no interest

    ____ 2 Average interest

    ____ 3 Fascinated by certain mechanical things

41. (Age 3–5) How does child usually react to being interrupted at what it is doing?
  _____ 1 Rarely or never gets upset
  _____ 2 Sometimes gets mildly upset; rarely very upset
  _____ 3 Typically gets very upset

42. (Age 3–5) Will the child readily accept new articles of clothing (shoes, coats, etc.)?
  _____ 1 Usually resists new clothes
  _____ 2 Doesn't seem to mind, or enjoys them

43. (Age 3–5) Is child upset by certain things that are not "right" (like crack in wall, spot on rug, books leaning in bookcase, broken rung on chair, pipe held and not smoked)?
  _____ 1 Not especially
  _____ 2 Yes, such things often upset him greatly
  _____ 3 Not sure

44. (Age 3–5) Does child adopt complicated "rituals" that make him very upset if not followed (such as putting many dolls to bed in a certain order, taking exactly the same route between two places, dressing according to a precise pattern, or insisting that only certain words be used in a given situation)?
  _____ 1 Yes, definitely
  _____ 2 Not sure
  _____ 3 No

45. (Age 3–5) Does child get very upset if certain things he is used to are changed (like furniture or toy arrangement, or certain doors which must be left open or shut)?
    _____ 1 No
    _____ 2 Yes, definitely
    _____ 3 Slightly true

46. (Age 3–5) Is the child destructive?
    _____ 1 Yes, this is definitely a problem
    _____ 2 Not deliberately or severely destructive
    _____ 3 Not especially destructive

47. (Age 3–5) Is the child unusually physically pliable (can be led easily; melts into your arms)?
    _____ 1 Yes
    _____ 2 Seems normal in this way
    _____ 3 Definitely not pliable

48. (Age 3–5) Which single description, or combination of two descriptions, best characterizes the child?
    _____ 1 Hyperactive, constantly moving, changes quickly from one thing to another
    _____ 2 Watches television quietly for long periods
    _____ 3 Sits for long periods, staring into space or playing repetitively with objects, without apparent purpose
    _____ 4 Combination of 1 and 2
    _____ 5 Combination of 2 and 3
    _____ 6 Combination of 1 and 3

49. (Age 3–5) Does the child seem to want to be liked?
    _____ 1 Yes, unusually so
    _____ 2 Just normally so
    _____ 3 Indifferent to being liked; happiest
           when left alone

50. (Age 3–5) Is child sensitive and/or affectionate?
    _____ 1 Is sensitive to criticism and affectionate
    _____ 2 Is sensitive to criticism, *not* affectionate
    _____ 3 Not sensitive to criticism, is
           affectionate
    _____ 4 Not sensitive to criticism *nor*
           affectionate

51. (Age 3–5) Is it possible to direct child's attention to an
    object some distance away or out a window?
    _____ 1 Yes, no special problem
    _____ 2 He rarely sees things very far out of
           reach
    _____ 3 He examines things with fingers and
           mouth only

52. (Age 3–5) Do people consider the child especially
    attractive?
    _____ 1 Yes, very good-looking child
    _____ 2 No, just average
    _____ 3 Faulty in physical appearance

53. (Age 3–5) Does the child look up at people (meet their
    eyes) when they are talking to him?.
    _____ 1 Never, or rarely
    _____ 2 Only with parents
    _____ 3 Usually does

54. (Age 3–5) Does the child take an adult by the wrist to use adult's hand (to open door, get cookies, turn on TV, etc.)?

_____ 1 Yes, this is typical

_____ 2 Perhaps, or rarely

_____ 3 No

55. (Age 3–5) Which set of terms best describes the child?

_____ 1 Confused, self-concerned, perplexed, dependent, worried

_____ 2 Aloof, indifferent, self-contented, remote

56. (Age 3–5) Is the child extremely fearful?

_____ 1 Yes, of strangers or certain people

_____ 2 Yes, of certain animals, noises, or objects

_____ 3 Yes, of 1 and 2 above

_____ 4 Only normal fearfulness

_____ 5 Seems unusually bold and free of fear

_____ 6 Child ignores or is unaware of fearsome objects

57. (Age 3–5) Does he fall or get hurt in running or climbing?

_____ 1 Tends toward falling or injury

_____ 2 Average in this way

_____ 3 Never, or almost never, exposes self to falling

_____ 4 Surprisingly safe despite active climbing, swimming, etc.

58. (Age 3–5) Is there a problem in that the child hits, pinches, bites or otherwise injures *himself* or *others*?
    _____ 1 Yes, self only
    _____ 2 Yes, others only
    _____ 3 Yes, self and others
    _____ 4 No (not a problem)

59. At what age did the child say his first words (even if later stopped talking)?
    _____ 1 Has never used words
    _____ 2 8–12 months
    _____ 3 13–15 months
    _____ 4 16–24 months
    _____ 5 2 years–3 years
    _____ 6 3 years–4 years
    _____ 7 After 4 years old
    _____ 8 Don't know

59a. On lines below list child's first six words (as well as you can remember them)
    _____ _____ _____
    _____ _____ _____

60. (Before age 5) Did the child start to talk, then become silent again for a week or more?
    _____ 1 Yes, but later talked again (age
            stopped _____,
            duration _____)
    _____ 2 Yes, but never started again (age stopped
            _____)
    _____ 3 No, continued to talk, or never began talking

61. (Before age 5) Did the child start to talk, then stop, and begin to whisper instead, for a week or more?

   ____ 1 Yes, but later talked again (age stopped _____, duration _____)

   ____ 2 Yes, still only whispers (age stopped talking _____)

   ____ 3 Now doesn't even whisper (stopped talking _____, stopped whispering _____)

   ____ 4 No, continued to talk, or never began talking

62. (Age 1–5) How well could the child *pronounce* his first words when learning to speak, and how well could he pronounce difficult words between 3 and 5?

   ____ 1 Too little speech to tell, or other answer

   ____ 2 Average or below average pronunciation of first words ("wabbit," etc.), and also poor at 3–5

   ____ 3 Average or below on first words, unusually good at 3–5

   ____ 4 Unusually good on first words, average or below at 3–5

   ____ 5 Unusually good on first words, and also at 3–5

63. (Age 3–5) Is the child's vocabulary (the number of things he can name or point to accurately) greatly out of proportion to his ability to "communicate" (to answer questions or tell you something)?

   _____ 1 He can *point* to many objects I name, but doesn't speak or "communicate"

   _____ 2 He can correctly *name* many objects, but not "communicate"

   _____ 3 Ability to "communicate" is pretty good—about what you would expect from the number of words he knows

   _____ 4 Doesn't use or understand words

64. When the child spoke his first sentences, did he surprise you by using words he had not used individually before?

   _____ 1 Yes (any examples? _____)

   _____ 2 No

   _____ 3 Not sure

   _____ 4 Too little speech to tell

65. How did child refer to *himself* on first learning to talk?

   _____ 1 "(John) fall down," or "Baby (or Boy) fall down"

   _____ 2 "Me fall down," or "I fall down"

   _____ 3 "(He, Him, She, or Her) fall down"

   _____ 4 "You fall down"

   _____ 5 Any combination of 1, 2, and/or 3

   _____ 6 Combination of 1 and 4

   _____ 7 No speech or too little speech as yet

66. (Age 3–5) Does child repeat phrases or sentences that he has heard in the past (maybe using a hollow, parrotlike voice), what is said having little or no relation to the situation?
    ___ 1 Yes, definitely, except voice not hollow or parrotlike
    ___ 2 Yes, definitely, including peculiar voice tone
    ___ 3 Not sure
    ___ 4 No
    ___ 5 Too little speech to tell

67. (Before age 5) Can the child answer a simple question such as "What is your first name?"; "Why did Mommy spank Billy?"
    ___ 1 Yes, can answer such questions adequately
    ___ 2 No, uses speech, but can't answer questions
    ___ 3 Too little speech to tell

68. (Before age 5) Can the child understand what you say to him, judging from his ability to follow instructions or answer you?
    ___ 1 Yes, understands very well
    ___ 2 Yes, understands fairly well
    ___ 3 Understands a little, if you repeat and repeat
    ___ 4 Very little or no understanding

69. (Before age 5) If the child talks, do you feel he understands what he is saying?
_____ 1 Doesn't talk enough to tell
_____ 2 No, he is just repeating what he has heard with hardly any understanding
_____ 3 Not just repeating—he understands what he is saying, but not well
_____ 4 No doubt that he understands what he is saying

70. (Before age 5) Has the child used the word *"yes"*?
_____ 1 Has used *"yes"* fairly often and correctly
_____ 2 Seldom has used *"yes,"* but has used it
_____ 3 Has used sentences, but hasn't used word *"yes"*
_____ 4 Has used a number of other words or phrases, but hasn't used word *"yes"*
_____ 5 Has no speech, or too little speech to tell

71. (Age 3–5) Does the child typically say "yes" by repeating the same question he has been asked? (Example: You ask, "Shall we go for a walk, Honey?" and he indicates he does want to by saying "Shall we go for a walk, Honey?" or "Shall we go for a walk?")
_____ 1 Yes, definitely, does not say "yes" directly
_____ 2 No, would say "yes" or "okay" or similar answer
_____ 3 Not sure
_____ 4 Too little speech to say

72. (Before age 5) Has the child asked for something by using the same sentence *you* would use when you offer it to him? (Example: The child wants milk, so he says: "Do *you* want some milk?" or "*You* want some milk?")

   ____ 1 Yes, definitely (uses "You" instead of "I")

   ____ 2 No, would ask differently

   ____ 3 Not sure

   ____ 4 Not enough speech to tell

73. (Before age 5) Has the child used the word "I"?

   ____ 1 Has used "I" fairly often and correctly

   ____ 2 Seldom has used "I," but has used it correctly

   ____ 3 Has used sentences, but hasn't used the word "I"

   ____ 4 Has used a number of words or phrases, but hasn't used the word "I"

   ____ 5 Has used "I," but only where word "you" belonged

   ____ 6 Has no speech, or too little speech to tell

74. (Before age 5) How does the child usually say "no" or refuse something?

   ____ 1 He would just say "no"

   ____ 2 He would ignore you

   ____ 3 He would grunt and wave his arms

   ____ 4 He would use some rigid meaningful phrase (like "Don't want it!" or "No milk!" or "No walk!")

   ____ 5 Would use phrase having only private meaning like "Daddy go in car"

   ____ 6 Other, or too little speech to tell

75. (Before age 5) Has the child used one word or idea as a substitute for another, for a prolonged time? (Example: always says "catsup" to mean "red," or uses "penny" for "drawer" after seeing pennies in a desk drawer)

____ 1 Yes, definitely

____ 2 No

____ 3 Not sure

____ 4 Too little speech to tell

76. Knowing what you do now, at what age do you think you could have first detected the child's abnormal behavior? That is, when did detectable abnormal behavior actually begin? (Under "A," indicate when you *might* have; under "B" when you *did*.)

A		B
____ 1	In first 3 months	____
____ 2	4–6 months	____
____ 3	7–12 months	____
____ 4	13–24 months	____
____ 5	2 years–3 years	____
____ 6	3 years–4 years	____
____ 7	After 4th year	____

Parents' highest educational level (77 for father, 78 for mother)

77.   78.

77	78	
		1 Did not graduate high school
		2 High school graduate
		3 Post high school tech. training
		4 Some college
		5 College graduate
		6 Some graduate work
		7 Graduate degree (_____)

79. Indicate the child's nearest blood relatives, including parents, who have been in a mental hospital or who were known to have been seriously mentally ill or retarded. Consider *parents, siblings, grandparents, uncles,* and *aunts.*

If none, check here ☐

Relationship   Diagnosis (if known)

_____ 1_____ Schizophrenia __ Depressive__ Other _____
_____ 2_____   "   __   "   __   "   _____
_____ 3_____   "   __   "   __   "   _____
_____ 4_____   "   __   "   __   "   _____
_____ 5_____   "   __   "   __   "   _____

Appendix B:

Primer on Nutrition

CHILDREN ARE INDEED what they eat.

What they eat affects their learning ability, their health, and their growth.

A common mistake made by parents is to use food as a bribe, as a reward, or as a punishment. When you say to a child, "If you are good, you can have that piece of ice cream cake," you are using food to serve psychological needs but not physiological needs. A child's optimal nutrition is too important to be discarded in the interest of achieving some transitory act of compliance.

Control of diet, I have tried to stress, is absolutely vital in the treatment of severely disturbed or learning disabled children. Acute attention must be focused on the child's *internal environment* if we are to help him overcome his learning and behavioral impediments.

Many parents seem to feel that their control over what their children eat ends early and that they are little more than passive bystanders as the youngsters join the parade of junk food consumers. Admittedly, it takes resolve and dedication to see that a child eats properly.

Aside from the temptation of bribery, parents must resist giving in to a child who nags them to buy the products advertised on television. In addition, they should think more in terms of cooking fresh foods than in putting convenience foods on the table. When "eating out," they should lead the way to places serving more healthful fare than that dispensed in most fast-food outlets and by vending machines.

I am certainly not the first doctor to caution parents about "feeding your kids right." As someone so nutrition-oriented, I feel rewarded that more and more parents are seeing the wisdom of our counsel. In advising them to watch carefully what a child is eating, I also tell them to keep a timetable of *when* the child is eating. We then have both a nutritional profile of the child and an index to scheduling his meals and snacks so that he can function optimally on an even keel.

We can speak all we want of vitamins, minerals, protein, simple and complex carbohydrates, and the other nutrients requisite for the healthy child, but the child's garden of nutrition also needs water to grow. I think of water as a nutrient, because it provides minerals vital to life. Too rarely do we see youngsters drinking water, and I tell parents over and again that one liquid is not as good as another. There is no substitute for water; whatever other beverages a child may be consuming is irrelevant—and too often unhealthy.

I give each parent the following primer on nutrition. Most of the guidelines are as adaptable to the needs of the whole family as they are to improving the nutrition of the disordered child.

In general:

- Do not use white bread.

- Do not serve any food to which anyone in the family is allergic or even sensitive.

- Try to limit servings of red meat to one meal each week.

- Good protein sources are milk, cheese, fish, chicken, turkey, all beans, sprouts, and nuts. It is particularly important for the learning disabled child to have a sufficiency of protein and preferably at each meal of the day. An insufficiency will lower the level of the neurotransmitters in the brain and diminish brain activity.

- Soft cheeses have a lower fat content than hard cheeses; try to use soft cheeses (cottage, pot, farmer, ricotta).

- Eating cheese with bread produces a very *rapid* rise in blood glucose levels. Eating rice with beans produces a very *slow* rise in blood glucose levels. Eating pasta with beans produces a very *slow* rise in blood glucose levels. The slow rise in blood glucose levels is better.

Try to avoid these foods in your diet:

All white flour

Refined sugar

Excessive salting of food

Coffee, tea, and cola beverages

Chocolate

Foods containing additives, artificial flavors, colors, or preservatives

Try to include these foods:

Raw seeds—sunflower, pumpkin, or sesame

Raw nuts—especially walnuts, pecans, almonds, filberts, cashews, or peanuts

Raw fruits—fresh, unsprayed, washed, and scrubbed with a vegetable scrubbing brush (always preferable to canned or frozen)

Raw or steamed vegetables—many vegetables that are usually cooked can be eaten raw in salads: spinach, cauliflower, broccoli, beets, carrots, peppers, cabbages, onions. Seeds and nuts can be added to the salads. Dressings ought to be fresh and made of such ingredients as unsaturated oils, cider vinegar, fresh lemon juice, yogurt, garlic, and herbs. A salad should be eaten every day.

Yogurt—unflavored, enhanced with fresh fruit or nuts and seeds. Acidophilus cultured yogurts are best.

Cheese in moderation—cottage, cheddar, Swiss, farmer's, ricotta, or any other unprocessed cheese

Eggs—also in moderation

Whole grains and legumes—rice, millet, oats, barley, rye, wheat, beans (including soybeans)

Fish—small ones, such as trout, sole, red snapper, flounder. (They accumulate less mercury.)

Here's a sample menu for one day of good eating:

Breakfast—medium orange or half grapefruit; one slice of whole grain bread or toast; cooked cereal or that occasional egg

Lunch—large salad with lots of greens and a wide variety of fresh vegetables or fruits; cottage cheese; unsweetened fruit bars made of dried apricots, apples, pineapples, pears, dates, or raisins; nuts or seeds

Afternoon snack—milk or fruit juice; apples, carrot or celery sticks; nuts; cheese

Dinner—homemade soup; a moderate portion (three ounces) of lean meat, fish, or poultry; steamed fresh vegetables; baked potato; milk; fresh fruit

Bedtime snack—juice or hot carob cocoa

These foods are recommended:

Vegetables—asparagus, beets, broccoli, Brussels sprouts, cabbage, carrots, cauliflower, celery, cucumbers, eggplant, all legumes, onions, squash, string beans, turnips, leeks, watercress, endive, zucchinis

Fruits—apricots, avocados, bananas, berries, grapefruits, melons, oranges, peaches, pears, pineapples, tangerines, grapes. (If canned fruits are on your shopping list, look for the "no-sugar-added" variety.)

Juices—all fresh fruit and vegetable juices. (Again, if canned, select salt-free and sugar-free varieties.)

Desserts—unsweetened gelatin; raw, dried, or stewed
fruit; cheese; natural applesauce; fruit stuffed with nuts
or seeds; melon; fresh fruit salad; fruit compotes topped
with chopped nuts and unsweetened coconut; refrig-
erator-frozen popsicles made from a mix of juice and
yogurt

Foods High in Essential Nutrients

The Family of Vitamins

A
Carrots
Leafy green vegetables
Butter
Whole milk
Liver
Fish

B$_1$
Liver
Pork
Yeast
Organ meats
Whole grains
Wheat germ
Peanuts

B$_2$
Eggs
Liver
Yeast
Milk
Whole grains

Wheat germ
Poultry
Fish
Meats (lean pork)
Legumes

B$_3$
Yeast
Liver
Whole bran
Peanuts
Beans

B$_6$
Wheat germ
Kidneys
Liver
Ham
Wheat bran
Legumes
Cereals

B$_{12}$
Liver
Organ meats
Oysters
Salmon
Eggs
Beef

B$_{15}$
Brewer's yeast
Organ meats
Whole grains

C
Fresh citrus fruits
Berries
Broccoli
Tomatoes
Leafy green vegetables
Baked potatoes
Turnips

D
Milk
Cod liver oil
Egg yolk
Liver
Sardines, herring, salmon

E
Margarine
Wheat germ
Whole grains
Oats
Cottonseed and safflower oil
Cabbage
Spinach
Peanuts
Broccoli
Whole-wheat bread
Eggs

K
Cabbage
Kale
Spinach
Beef
Pork
Cauliflower
Tomatoes
Peas
Carrots

P
Green peppers
Tomatoes
Apricots
Rhubarb
Pulp and rind of citrus fruits

Protein

Eggs
Milk
Chicken
Pork
Soybeans
Beans
Peas
Nuts
Whole wheat

Cheese
Fish
Beef
Soy milk
Soy flour
Organ meats
Shellfish
Liver

Saturated Fats

Lard
Butter
Peanut butter
Organ meats
Legumes
Nuts
Salad oils

Cream
Cheese
Bacon
Pork
Beef
Fish
Whole milk

Polyunsaturated Fats

Margarine from safflower,
   corn, or soy oil
Corn oil
Safflower oil

Peanut oil
Soybean oil
Cottonseed oil

Fiber

Whole grains
Brown rice

Buckwheat
Oats

Bran   Millet
Whole wheat   Vegetables

Carbohydrates

Fruits   Legumes
Vegetables   Yams
Wheat products   Sweet and white potatoes

Foods with High Concentrations of Minerals

Magnesium

Soybeans   Whole corn
Soy flour   Beans
Clams   Nuts
Whole wheat   Wheat germ
Oatmeal   Cocoa
Raisins   Peas
Spinach   Brown rice

Sodium

Dried beef   Dried fish
Ham   Eggs
Canned corned beef   Carrots
Butter   Olives
Margarine   Cauliflower
Cheese   Canned vegetables and soups
Clams   Oatmeal
Shellfish and saltwater fish   Pickles
Oysters   Bacon

Sodium

Wheat breads
Salted crackers
Pretzels
Celery
Raisins
Beets
Beef
Sausage

Spinach
Turnips
Broccoli
Melons
Milk
Peanuts
Pumpkin

Calcium

Cream cheese
Cheese
Cow's milk
Bread
Eggs
Nuts
Cream
Legumes
Leafy green vegetables

Broccoli
Cauliflower
Chocolate
Cottage cheese
Spinach
Bran flakes
Celery
Oatmeal
Raisins

Iron

Liver
Organ meats
Eggs
Sweetbreads
Avocadoes
Dates
Beef
Spinach
Legumes
Oysters

Nuts
Parsley
Molasses
Raisins
Bran flakes
Wheat germ
Oatmeal
Mushrooms
Leafy green vegetables
Cereals

Copper

Calf liver
Beef liver
Oysters
Molasses
Mushrooms
Nuts
Lobster

Bran flakes
Cereals
Fruits
Leafy green vegetables
Meat
Brewer's yeast

Iodine

Cod liver oil
Iodized salt
Shellfish
Saltwater fish
Bacon
Agar
Eggs
Oats
Peaches
Butter
Lamb
Cottage cheese
Spinach

Freshwater fish
Applesauce
Bread
Celery
Asparagus
Bananas
Beef
Lemons
Olive oil
Canned pears
Potatoes
Cream
Corn

Manganese

Wheat bran
Blackberries
Graham bread
Barley
Rye bread
Bananas
Parsley
Buckwheat bread
Blueberries

Nuts
Oatmeal
Coconut
Beets
Lettuce
Cocoa
Split peas, dried
Turnip greens

Zinc

Oysters

Commercial casein

Cereals

Meat

Vegetables

Cow's milk

Pantothenic Acid

Liver

Organ meats

Eggs

Yeast

Potassium

Leafy green vegetables

Nuts

Vegetable juice

Molasses

Peanuts

Bananas

Spinach

Potatoes

Oatmeal

Mushrooms

Turnips

Carrots

Figs

Legumes

Cocoa

Olives

Raisins

Parsnips

Apples

Wheat germ

Rye flour

Sweet potatoes

Beets

Pumpkin

Coconuts

Chloride

Butter

Rye bread

Oysters

Molasses

Eggs

Turnips

Wheat germ

Sardines

Clams

Cheese

Graham crackers

Celery

Bananas

Beans

Breast milk

Salmon

Yogurt

Phosphorus

Whole wheat	Soy flour
Oatmeal	Beans
Nuts	Peas
Brown rice	Cheese
Eggs	Bran flakes
Yeast	Ham
Cottage cheese	Fish
Turkey	Liver
Pork	Chicken
Lamb	Lobster
Beef	

Additives Commonly Used in Foods and Beverages

Sodium nitrite
Gum arabic
Saccharin
Sodium acid pyrophosphate
FD&C red No. 2
FD&C yellow No. 5
Monosodium glutamate (MSG)
Heptyl paraben
Sodium propionate
Propylene glycol alginate
Sodium benzoate
Disodium EDTA
Butylated hydroxyanisole (BHA)
Butylated hydroxytoluene (BHT)
Brominated vegetable oil
All artificial flavors
All artificial colors

Products Containing Artificial Flavorings, Colorings, and Other Additives

Ice cream
Margarine
Gin and all distilled beverages (except vodka)
Cake mixes
Bakery goods (except plain bread)
Jello
Candies
Cider and cider vinegars
Wine and wine vinegars
Presweetened drink mixes
Soda pop (all soft drinks)
All tea
Beer
Diet drinks and supplements

Cloves
Oil of wintergreen
Toothpaste and toothpowder
Mint flavors
Lozenges
Mouthwash
Jam or jelly
Luncheon meats (salami, bologna, etc.)
Frankfurters (hot dogs)

Note: Check all labels of prepared foods for additives and try to avoid those that are ridden with chemicals.

Natural Sources of Salicylates

Almonds
Apples
Apricots
Blackberries
Cherries
Currants
Gooseberries
Grapes or raisins
Nectarines

Oranges
Peaches
Plums
Prunes
Raspberries
Strawberries
Cucumbers and pickles
Tomatoes

Foods Containing Milk

Baking powder biscuits
Baker's bread
Bavarian cream
Bisques
Blanc mange
Butter
Buttermilk
Butter sauces
Cakes
Candies
Chocolate
Cocoa drinks, mixtures
Chowders
Cookies
Cream
Creamed foods
Cream sauces
Cheeses
Curds
Custards
Doughnuts
Scrambled eggs and scalloped dishes
Foods prepared au gratin
Food fried in butter:
    fish
    poultry
    beef
    pork

Flour mixtures
Fritters
Gravies
Hamburgers
Hash
Hard sauces
Hot cakes
Ice creams
Junket
Mashed potatoes
Malted milk
Ovaltine
Ovomalt
Meat loaf
Cooked sausages
Milk chocolate
Omelets
Pie crust made with milk
    products
Prepared flour mixtures such
    as:
    biscuits
    cake
    cookies
    doughnuts
    muffins
    pancake
    pie crust
    waffles

Foods Containing Milk

Rarebits
Salad dressings
Sherbets
Soda crackers
Souffles

Soups
Spumoni
Whey
Zweiback

The Presence of Wheat

Beverages
Cocomalt
Beer
Gin (any drink with grain-
    neutral spirits)
Malted milk
Ovaltine
Postum
Whiskies

Breads
Biscuits
Crackers
Muffins
Popovers
Pretzels
Rolls
Corn bread
Gluten bread
Graham bread
Pumpernickel
Soy wheat
Rye (rye products are *not*
    entirely free of wheat)

Cereals
Bran flakes
Corn flakes
Cream of Wheat
Crackels
Pep
Pettijohns
Puffed Wheat
Ralston's wheat cereal
Rice Krispies
Shredded Wheat
Triscuits
Wheatena
Other malted cereals

Flours
Buckwheat flour
Corn flour
Graham flour
Lima bean flour
Patent flour
Rye flour
White flour
Whole wheat flour
Gluten flour

Pastries and Desserts
Cakes
Cookies
Doughnuts
Frozen Pies
Pies
Chocolate candy
Candy bars
Puddings

Wheat products
Bread
Dumplings
Macaroni
Noodles
Rusks
Spaghetti
Vermicelli
Zweiback

Miscellaneous
Bouillon cubes
Chocolate candy
Chocolate (except bitter cocoa
    and bitter chocolate)

Cooked mixed meat dishes
Fats used for frying foods that
    are rolled in flour
Gravies
Griddle cakes
Hot cakes
Ice cream cones
Meat rolled in flour
Most of the cooked sausages
    (weiner, bologna, liverwurst,
    luncheon ham, hamburger)
Matzos
Mayonnaise
Pancake mixtures
Sauces
Synthetic pepper
Some yeasts
Thickening in ice creams
Waffles
Wheat cakes
Wheat germ

Foods, Beverages, and Products Containing Corn, Corn Syrup, and Corn Sugar

Adhesives
Envelopes
Stamps
Stickers
Tapes
Ales
Aspirin and other tablets
Bacon
Baking mixes such as:
   biscuits
   pie crusts
   doughnuts
   pancake mixes
Baking powders
Batters for frying
Beers
Beverages (carbonated)
Bleached wheat flour
Bourbon and other whiskies
Breads and pastries
Cakes
Candles
Catsups
Cheeses
Chili
Chop suey
Instant coffee
Cookies
Corn flakes
Cough syrups

Cream pies
Milk in paper cartons
Oleomargarine
Peanut butters
Canned peas
Powdered sugar
Preserves
Puddings, custards
Rice (coated)
Salad dressings
Sandwich spreads
Sauces for meats and sundaes
Sherbets
Dates (confection)
Deep-fat frying mixtures
French dressing
Fritos
Frostings
Fruits (canned and frozen)
Fruit juices
Frying fats
Gelatin dessert (capsules)
Glucose products
Graham crackers
Grape juice
Gravies
Grits
Gum, chewing
Hams (cured/tenderized)
Ice creams

Inhalants (bath and body powders)
Popcorn
Starch
Jams, jellies
Meats (bologna, sausage)
Similac
String beans (canned and frozen)
Soups (creamed and vegetables)
Soy bean milks
Sugar, powdered
Syrups
Commercial preparations:
cartose
glucose

Karo
Puretose
Sweetose
Talcums
Teas, instant
Toothpaste
Tortillas
Vegetables (canned, creamed, frozen)
Vanilla
Vinegar, distilled
Vitamins (tablets, lozenges, suppositories, capsules)
Wines (some American wines are corn-free)
Zest

Foods Containing Egg

Baking powders
Batters for French frying
Bavarian cream
Boiled dressings
Bouillons
Breads
Breaded foods
Cakes
Cake flours
Eggs
Fritters
Frostings
French toast

Griddle cakes
Glazed rolls
Hamburger mix
Hollandaise sauce
Ices
Ice cream
Icings
Macaroons
Malted cocoa drinks such as:
Ovaltine
Ovomalt (and many others)
Macaroni
Marshmallows

217

Foods Containing Egg

Mayonnaise
Meat loaf
Meat jellies
Meat molds
Meringues (French torte)
Noodles
Pastas
Pancakes
Pancake flours
Patties
Puddings
Pretzels
Quiche
Salad dressings

Sauces
Sausages
Sherbets
Soufflés
Spaghetti
Spanish creams
Soups:
    noodle
    mock turtle
    consommés
Tartar sauce
Timbales
Waffles
Waffle mixes

Appendix C:

Healthful, Tasty Favorites of Kids

THE FOLLOWING RECIPES, which are for the most part quite simple, have been designed for children whose diets must be revised to eliminate sugar, additives, and other undesirable components. They are palatable and nutritious, without looking or tasting "health foody."

SUBSTANTIAL DISHES

DYNAMITE PANCAKES

If you make the batter the night before, your pancakes will not only be more flavorful, but the pancakes could be said to be almost an "instant" breakfast. Any leftover batter will keep tightly covered for about a week in the refrigerator.

2   eggs
2   cups milk
2   tablespoons honey*

*Foods and beverages containing honey should not be given to children less than a year old.

1¼	cups whole wheat pastry flour
1	tablespoon baking powder
2	tablespoons polyunsaturated oil
¼	teaspoon vanilla extract
¾	cup rolled oats
¾	cup walnuts
¼	cup sunflower seeds
¼	cup sesame seeds
¼	cup wheat germ
¼	cup bran
1	apple, shredded

Combine the eggs, milk, and honey in a large bowl. Sift the flour with the baking powder and add to the egg mixture with the oil and vanilla. Blend well before mixing in the oats, nuts, sunflower and sesame seeds, wheat germ, bran, and apple. Refrigerate overnight.

To cook, spoon the batter onto a hot griddle, which has been lightly greased with corn oil, and cook until browned. Then turn and cook on the other side.

For a topping, try unsweetened applesauce instead of over-sweetened syrups.

Makes 4 servings.

YUMMY BREAKFAST IN A JIF

For the mom and the child in a hurry.

1	cup cold milk
1	egg
3	tablespoons undiluted orange juice concentrate
½	banana
1	heaping teaspoonful of wheat germ
1	teaspoonful of protein powder

Put the ingredients in the container of a blender and blend at high speed until frothy. Serve immediately. If a thicker shake is desired, use more banana.

Makes 1 serving.

HONEY OF A PEANUT BUTTER SANDWICH

Nowadays almost everybody lives within easy access to a health food store or nutrition center that offers pure peanut butter without oil, salt, and preservatives.

2	slices whole grain bread
¼	cup peanut butter
½	banana, thinly sliced
1	tablespoon honey

Spread 1 slice of the bread with the peanut butter. Cover the peanut butter with the banana slices. Dribble the honey over the peanut butter and banana slices. Top with the other slice of bread and cut the sandwich in half on the diagonal.

Makes 1 serving.

BLACK BEAN SOUP

1	large onion, chopped
3	tablespoons corn or safflower oil
10	cups water or vegetable stock
6	cups drained cooked black beans
2	carrots, chopped
2	raw, unpeeled potatoes, chopped
6	whole black peppercorns
2	bay leaves
	Pinch of dried basil
1	teaspoon soy sauce
	Juice of 1 lemon

In a large soup kettle, sauté the onion in the oil. Add the water or vegetable stock and beans and bring to a boil. Simmer the soup for ½ hour; then add the chopped carrots and potatoes, peppercorns, bay leaves, and basil. Simmer for 15 minutes and add the soy sauce. Stir well. Right before serving, when the vegetables are tender, stir in the lemon juice.

Makes 10 or more servings.

CHICKEN SOUP PLUS

1	3-pound chicken, cut up
6	cups cold water
2	chicken bouillon cubes
1	bay leaf
2	celery stalks, sliced
1	large onion, chopped
6	carrots, sliced
1	cup uncooked brown rice

Put the chicken in a large saucepan. Add the water, bouillon cubes, and bay leaf. Bring to a boil. Simmer for 1 hour, or until the chicken is tender. Remove the chicken from the stock. Let the chicken and stock cool. Then remove the skin and bones from the chicken and discard them. Cut the chicken meat into bite-sized pieces.

Reheat the broth and add the vegetables and rice. Simmer for 35 minutes. Add the chicken pieces and cook for 15 minutes longer.

Makes 6 servings.

CHILI CON CARNE SUPREME

1	tablespoon vegetable oil
2	pounds very lean, coarsely ground beef
2	cups onion, finely chopped
2	tablespoons garlic, finely chopped
1	cup green pepper, finely chopped
1	cup celery, finely chopped
1	tablespoon crumbled dried oregano
2	bay leaves
2	teaspoons cumin
1	tablespoon chili powder
3	cups canned tomatoes with tomato paste
1	cup beef broth
1	cup water
½	teaspoon hot red pepper flakes
2	cups drained canned kidney beans
1	tablespoon honey
3	tablespoons wheat germ

Heat the oil in large heavy kettle. Add the meat and cook, chopping down and stirring with the side of a heavy metal kitchen spoon to break up any lumps.

Add the onion, garlic, green pepper, celery, oregano, bay leaves, cumin, and chili powder. Stir to blend well.

Add the tomatoes, broth, water, and hot red pepper flakes. Bring to a boil and cook, stirring often, for about 20 minutes. Add the beans, honey, and wheat germ and cook for 10 minutes longer. Serve in hot bowls, with shredded cheddar cheese, if desired.

Makes 8 or more servings.

MEXICALI SOUFFLÉ

1	large onion, chopped
2	tablespoons corn oil
3	cups *cooked* brown rice
2	cups cooked corn
1½	cups grated cheddar cheese
	Pinch of chili powder
1	teaspoon ground cumin
3	eggs, separated
1½	cups cottage cheese, creamed style

Preheat the oven to 375 degrees.

Sauté the onion in the oil until the onion is soft. Remove from the heat and add the brown rice, cooked corn, 1 cup of the cheddar cheese, and the spices.

Beat the egg yolks into the cottage cheese; then incorporate the mixture into the rice mixture.

Beat the egg whites until stiff. Then fold them gently but thoroughly into the rice mixture. Turn the mixture into a greased casserole and bake for 20 minutes. Sprinkle the remaining cheddar cheese on top and bake for 15 to 20 minutes longer, or until the soufflé is set.

Makes 4 servings.

QUICK ZUCCHINI PIZZA

1   cup grated raw zucchini
1   egg, beaten
3   ounces mozzarella cheese, grated
1   tablespoon wheat germ
1   tablespoon whole wheat flour
4   tablespoons tomato sauce, preferably homemade from
       fresh tomatoes
       Pinch of Italian herbs
       Pinch of garlic powder
1   sweet red or green pepper, chopped
 ½   onion, chopped
4   fresh mushrooms, sliced

Preheat the oven to 350 degrees.

Combine the zucchini, egg, 1 ounce of the mozzarella cheese, wheat germ, and whole wheat flour in a bowl. Then spread the batter in a greased 8-inch-square baking pan. Bake for 25 minutes.

While the crust is baking, combine the tomato sauce, herbs, garlic powder, pepper, onion, and mushrooms in a bowl.

Spread the mixture over the baked crust in the pan and sprinkle the remaining 2 ounces of mozzarella on top. Return the pan to the oven and bake for 25 minutes longer.

Makes 2 servings.

SNACKS

AFTER-SCHOOL POPCORN SNACK

This is a nutritious pickup for your child and his pals. The cheese eliminates the need for salt.

2   cups unsalted freshly popped corn
4   tablespoons grated cheddar cheese
½   cup unsalted shelled peanuts
       Grated Parmesan or Romano cheese

Toss the popped corn with the cheddar cheese and peanuts; then sprinkle with the Parmesan or Romano cheese and toss again.

Makes 4 servings.

PEANUT BUTTER KNOCKOUTS

These make a great addition to the after-school cookie jar. They are so nutritious that a few of them could almost substitute for a lunch or dinner.

1½ cups whole wheat pastry flour
½ cup soy flour
½ cup wheat germ
1 cup rolled oats
1 teaspoon ground cinnamon
½ cup corn oil
½ cup peanut butter
½ cup honey
2 tablespoons water
1 teaspoon vanilla extract
½ cup raisins
½ cup grated coconut

Preheat the oven to 350 degrees.

Combine the flours, wheat germ, oats, and cinnamon in a bowl. Set aside.

In a large mixing bowl, cream the oil with the peanut butter. Add the honey, water, and vanilla; then stir in the flour mixture. Fold in the raisins and coconut.

Drop the batter by teaspoonfuls onto lightly greased baking sheets. Flatten each cookie with a fork, making a crisscross design. Bake for 10 to 12 minutes. Remove to wire racks to cool.

Makes about 4 dozen cookies.

PINEAPPLE FINGER GELATIN

Children love finger foods.

3   envelopes unflavored gelatin
1   12-ounce can frozen pineapple juice concentrate, thawed
1½ cups water

Soften the gelatin in the pineapple juice for a few minutes. Bring the water to a boil; then add the juice and gelatin mixture and stir until the gelatin has dissolved. Remove the pan from the heat and pour the mixture into a lightly greased 9- by 13-inch baking pan. Chill until firm. Cut into squares and refrigerate in a tightly covered container.

Makes 12 servings.

SNOW CONES

Put several ice cubes and ½ cup water into the container of a blender. Process, turning the blender on and off to achieve a snow-like consistency.

Scoop the "snow" into a paper cup; then pour over it 2 tablespoons of thawed frozen orange juice or grape juice concentrate.

Makes 1 serving.

TRAIL MIX

A highly energizing after-school snack, as well as a great pick-me-up literally "on the trail" (hiking, biking, jogging, etc.).

6	dried apple slices, chopped
½	pound banana chips
¼	cup dried chopped apricots
¼	cup dried chopped pineapple
½	cup dry-roasted peanuts
¼	cup dry-roasted cashews
¼	cup sesame seeds
1	cup dried unsweetened coconut flakes
1	cup chopped dates
1	cup shelled sunflower seeds
¼	cup wheat germ

Mix all the ingredients together in a bowl. Store in a tightly covered container in a cool place.

Makes about 6 cups.

HEALTHY, TASTY, SANDWICHY SQUASH BREAD

2½	cups water
1	cup cornmeal
2	tablespoons margarine
1	tablespoon honey, unsulfured molasses, or maple syrup
1	tablespoon sea salt
1	tablespoon active dry yeast

1½ cups lukewarm mashed butternut squash
1   cup unbleached flour
7   cups whole wheat flour

Bring 2 cups of the water to a boil and pour it over the cornmeal. Add the margarine, honey, and sea salt. Beat with a wire whisk or wooden spoon until the mixture is smooth. Set aside to cool.

Dissolve the yeast in the remaining ½ cup water. Add the dissolved yeast to the cooled cornmeal mixture along with the butternut squash. Stir to blend well.

Add the unbleached flour and 3 cups of the whole wheat flour and beat for 3 minutes with a wooden spoon. Add the remaining whole wheat flour, 1 cup at a time, until the dough is no longer sticky.

Turn out the dough onto a floured board and knead it for 10 minutes, using only as much additional flour as needed to keep the dough from sticking to the board.

Transfer the dough to an oiled bowl and turn it to oil the top. Cover the bowl and let the dough rise in a warm place, away from drafts, until it has doubled.

Punch down the dough and knead it briefly on a floured surface. Divide the dough in half and shape each half into a loaf. Transfer the loaves to buttered 9- by 5- by 3-inch loaf pans. Cover the pans and let the dough rise until it has doubled.

Preheat the oven to 400 degrees. Bake the loaves for about 55 minutes, or until they sound hollow when tapped on the bottom of the loaf.

Makes 2 loaves.

DESSERTS AND DRINKS
DELUXE CARROT CAKE

Cake

4	eggs
1½	cups honey
1½	cups corn or safflower oil
2	cups whole wheat flour
¼	cup wheat germ
2	teaspoons baking soda, or 1 teaspoon baking soda and 2 teaspoons baking powder
½	teaspoon salt
2	teaspoons ground cinnamon
½	cup unsweetened orange juice
3	cups grated raw carrots
½	cup unsweetened flaked coconut
1	cup chopped walnuts
½	cup raisins
½	cup drained crushed pineapple

Frosting

1 or 2	8-ounce packages cream cheese (depending on thickness desired), softened
	Honey to taste
1	teaspoon vanilla extract
	Milk

To prepare the cake, preheat the oven to 300 degrees.
Beat the eggs and add the honey. Add the oil and mix well.
Combine the flour, wheat germ, baking soda, salt, cinnamon, and orange juice and add the mixture to the egg mixture. Stir in the carrots, coconut, walnuts, raisins, and pineapple. Pour the batter into a 9- by 13-inch baking pan and bake for

45 minutes, or until a toothpick inserted in the center of the cake comes out clean. Cool the cake in a pan on a wire rack.

To prepare the frosting, beat the softened cream cheese until it is fluffy. Add the honey, vanilla, and enough milk to make a spreadable consistency.

Spread the frosting on the cooled cake and cut into squares.

Makes 12 servings.

GINGERBREAD

This is delicious by itself or topped with unsweetened yogurt or applesauce.

1¾ cups whole wheat flour
½   cup soy flour
½   teaspoon salt
1   teaspoon baking soda
2   teaspoons baking powder
1   tablespoon grated fresh gingerroot
2   eggs, beaten
⅓   cup corn or safflower oil
1   cup unsulfured molasses
¾   cup hot water

Preheat the oven to 325 degrees.

Put the flours, salt, baking soda, baking powder, and grated gingerroot into a mixing bowl. Stir to blend.

In another bowl, mix together the eggs, oil, molasses, and water. Add the liquid mixture to the dry mixture and blend with a few swift strokes. Pour the batter into a well-oiled 9-inch-square baking pan and bake for 30 to 35 minutes, or until a toothpick inserted in the center of the cake comes out clean. Cool the cake in the pan on a wire rack.

Makes 9 servings.

SUPER-DUPER COFFEE CAKE

1	cup whole wheat flour
1	teaspoon baking powder
¼	cup butter, softened
¼	cup honey
1	egg
¼	cup milk
1	teaspoon lemon juice
1	tablespoon grated lemon rind
½	cup raisins

Preheat the oven to 350 degrees.

Combine the flour and baking powder and set aside.

Cream together the butter and honey; then beat in the egg. Gradually blend the flour mixture into the butter mixture, alternating with the milk and lemon juice. Mix in the lemon rind and raisins.

Pour the batter into a well-oiled 8- by 4-inch loaf pan and bake for 35 minutes, or until a toothpick inserted in the center of the cake comes out clean. Cool the cake in the pan on a wire rack.

Makes 8 servings.

PEANUT BUTTER BROWNIES

½   cup oil
½   cup carob powder
½   cup peanut butter
½   cup honey
1   tablespoon blackstrap molasses
4   eggs, beaten
¾   cup whole wheat pastry flour
1   cup chopped walnuts

Preheat the oven to 350 degrees.

Pour the oil into a bowl and stir in the carob powder. Add the peanut butter, honey, molasses, eggs, flour, and walnuts, one ingredient at a time, stirring thoroughly after each addition.

Pour the batter into a lightly oiled 8-inch-square baking pan. Bake for about 25 minutes; then cool in the pan on a wire rack. Cut into squares to serve.

Makes 9 servings.

FRUITED POPSICLES

1   cup skim milk
1   envelope unflavored gelatin
¼   cup honey
1½   cups unsweetened orange, grape, or pineapple juice
1   egg white

Pour the milk into the container of a blender. Add the gelatin and let it soften for a few minutes before adding the remaining ingredients. Blend thoroughly.

235

Pour the mixture into popsicle molds and insert a popsicle stick into each mold. Freeze until firm. Then unmold and store in the freezer in a tightly closed plastic bag.

Makes 6 popsicles.

BANANA POPSICLES

6 firm but ripe bananas
½ teaspoon vitamin C crystals
¼ cup warm water
3 tablespoons honey
½ cup granola crumbs or crushed corn flakes

Peel the bananas and insert a wooden stick or plastic skewer in the end of each one. Freeze the bananas in a single layer on a baking sheet for ½ hour.

Dissolve the vitamin C crystals in the warm water. Add the honey and stir to mix well.

Roll the bananas in the honey mixture to moisten and coat them. Then roll each banana in the granola crumbs or crushed corn flakes. Freeze in a single layer on a baking sheet until firm. Any leftover popsicles can be stored in the freezer in a tightly closed plastic bag.

Makes 6 popsicles.

BANANA MILK SHAKE

½   cup milk
½   cup unsweetened orange juice
1   banana
1   tablespoon wheat germ
2   ice cubes

Put all the ingredients into the container of a blender. Cover and blend until smooth.

Makes 1 serving.

Bibliography

Adams, Ruth, and Frank Murray, eds. *Body, Mind and the B Vitamins.* New York: Larchmont Books, 1972.
———. *Megavitamin Therapy.* New York: Larchmont Books, 1973.
Adler, Sol. "Megavitamin Treatment for Behaviorally Disturbed and Learning Disabled Children." *Journal of Learning Disabilities,* Vol. 12, No. 10 (December 1979).
———. "Behavior Management: A Nutritional Approach to the Behaviorally Disordered and Learning Disabled Child." *Journal of Learning Disabilities,* Vol. 11, No. 12 (December 1978).
American Council on Science and Health. "Food Additives and Hyperactivity." (January 1982).
Associated Press. "Study Cites Sharp Increase in Breast Feeding." *The New York Times,* March 25, 1984.
Associated Press. "Indoor Pollution Is High." *The New York Times,* March 29, 1984.
Bachman, Joan, and Philip Firestone. "A Review of Psychopharmacological and Behavior Approaches to the Treat-

ment of Hyperactive Children." *American Journal of Orthopsychiatry*, Vol. 49, No. 3 (July 1979).

"Back to Reality the Megavitamin Way." *Medical World News*, September 24, 1971.

Balkwell, Carolyn, and Charles F. Halverson, Jr. "The Hyperactive Child as a Source of Stress in the Family: Consequences and Suggestions for Intervention." *Family Relations*, October 1980.

Bechtel, Stefan. "The Untwisting of Tongues." *Prevention*, September 1982.

Benowica, Robert J. *Vitamins & You.* New York: Berkley Books, 1981.

Boullin, D. J., M. Coleman, and R. A. O'Brien. "Abnormalities in Platelet 5-Hydroxytryptamine Efflux in Patients with Infantile Autism." *Nature*, No. 226 (1970), p. 371.

————, and B. Rimland. "Laboratory Predictions of Infantile Autism Based on 5-Hydroxytryptamine Efflux from Blood Platelets and Their Correlation with the Rimland E-2 Score." *Journal of Autism and Childhood Schizophrenia*, Vol. 1, No. 1 (1971), pp. 63–71.

Bremner, Robert H., ed. *Children and Youth in America: A Documentary History, Vol. 1 (1600–1865).* Cambridge, MA: Harvard University Press, 1970.

Brin, Geri. "Finding the Right Pediatrician." *New York*, May 10, 1982.

Brody, Jane. "The Importance of Dietary Control—Getting Children to Eat Right." *The New York Times*, June 16, 1982.

Bronfenbrenner, U. "Dampening the Unemployability Explosion." *Saturday Review*, January 4, 1969.

Brutten, Milton, Sylvia O. Richardson, and Charles Mangel. *Something's Wrong with My Child: A Parents' Book About*

Children with Learning Disabilities. New York: Harcourt Brace Jovanovich, Inc., 1973.

Bryce-Smith, D., and H. A. Waldron. "Lead Pollution, Disease, and Behavior." *Community Health,* June 1968.

———. "Lead Poisoning." *Chemistry in Britain,* Vol. 7, No. 54 (1971).

Buckley, R. E. "Nutrition, Metabolism, Brain Functions, and Learning." *Academic Therapy,* Vol. 12, No. 3 (1977), pp. 321–326.

Caprio, R. J., H. L. Margulis, and M. M. Joselow. "Lead Absorption in Children and Its Relationship to Urban Traffic Densities." *Archives of Environmental Health,* Vol. 28 (1974), pp. 195–197.

Colgan, Michael, and Lesley Colgan. "Do Nutrient Supplements and Dietary Changes Affect Learning and Emotional Reactions of Children with Learning Difficulties?: A Controlled Series of 16 Cases." *Nutrition and Health,* Vol. 3 (1984), pp. 69–77.

Conners, C. Keith, Charles H. Goyette, and Elisa B. Newman. "Dose-Time Effect of Artificial Colors in Hyperactive Children." *Journal of Learning Disabilities,* Vol. 13, No. 9 (November 1980).

Cousins, Norman. *Anatomy of an Illness.* New York: W.W. Norton, 1979.

D'Antonio, Michael. "Dr. Spock's Dr. Spock." *Newsday,* February 26, 1984.

Derdeyn, A. P. "Personality Development and Personality Disorders, with Emphasis on Anti-Social Personality." *Psychiatry Digest,* Vol. 10 (1974), p. 28.

Divoky, Diane, and Peter Schrag. *The Myth of the Hyperactive Child and Other Means of Child Control.* New York: Pantheon, 1975.

"Drug Linked to Growth Problems in Children." *Psychiatric News,* September 7, 1979.

Dullea, Georgia. "Parents, Children and Food." *The New York Times,* January 15, 1984.

Ellington, Careth. *The Shadow Children.* Chicago, IL.: Topaz Books, 1967.

Feingold, Ben F. *Why Your Child Is Hyperactive.* New York: Random House, 1975.

Finkel, A. *Hamilton and Hardy's Industrial Toxicology.* Boston: John Wright • PSG Inc., 1983.

Foy, Jessie Gray. *Gone Is Shadow's Child.* Plainfield, N.J.: Logos International, 1970.

Fredericks, Carlton. "Amphetamines or Diet for Emotionally Disturbed Children?" *Prevention,* April 1982.

Friedrich, Otto. "What Do Babies Know?" *Time,* August 15, 1983, pp. 52–59.

Gelenberg, Alan J. "Nutrition in Psychiatry." *Journal of Clinical Psychiatry,* Vol. 41, No. 10 (October 1980).

Golden, Gerald S. "Nonstandard Therapies in the Developmental Disabilities." *American Journal of Diseases of Children,* Vol. 134 (May 1980).

Gottlieb, Bill. "Bad Child or Bad Diet?" *Prevention,* July 1979.

Grant, Wilson W. "The Hyperactive Child: A Pediatrician's Program." *The Exceptional Parent,* October 1980.

Greenberg, Joel. "Unstable Emotions of Children Tied to Poor Diet." *The New York Times,* August 18, 1981.

Greenfeld, Josh. *A Child Called Noah.* New York: Holt, Rinehart and Winston, 1972.

Hamburg, David A. "Health and Behavior." *Science,* Vol. 217, No. 4558 (July 30, 1982).

Hawkins, David, and Linus Pauling, eds. *Orthomolecular Psychiatry, Treatment of Schizophrenia.* New York: W. H. Freeman and Co., 1973.

Hawley, C., and R. E. Buckley. "Food Dyes and Hyperkinetic Children." *Academic Therapy*, Vol. 10, No. 1 (1974), pp. 27–32.

Hillemann, Howard. "Maternal Malnutrition and Congenital Deformity." *Address*, March 17, 1958.

Hillman, Sheilah. *The Baby Checkup Book*. New York: Bantam Books, 1982.

Hoffer, Abram. Letter to colleagues re: bioflavonoids. June 21, 1983.

———, and Morton Walker. *Orthomolecular Nutrition: New Lifestyle for Super Good Health*. New Canaan, CT: Pivot Books, 1978.

Hoffman, M. S. "Early Indications of Learning Problems." *Academic Therapy*, Vol. 7, No. 1 (1971), pp. 23–35.

"Hyperactivity Drug Found to Stunt Boys' Growth." *Parents*, December 1979.

"Hyperactivity in the Classroom." *Special Education: Forward Trends*, Vol. 7, No. 2.

Jacobson, Mildred, and George Gasek. "Spotting and Helping the LD Child." *The Canadian Nurse*, June 1979.

Jani, S. N., and L. A. Jani. "Nutritional Deprivation and Learning Disabilities—An Appraisal." *Academic Therapy*, Vol. 11, No. 1 (1974), pp. 151–158.

Journal of Orthomolecular Psychiatry. Vols. 7–12. Saskatchewan, Canada: Canadian Schizophrenia Foundation, 1978–1983.

Kasowski, M. A., and W. J. Kasowski. "The Burden of Lead: How Much Is Safe?" *CMA Journal*, 114:573 (1976).

Kaufman, Barry Neil. *Son-Rise*. New York: Warner Books, 1977.

Kestembaum, Clarice J. "Children at Risk for Schizophrenia." *American Journal of Psychotherapy*, Vol. 34, No. 2 (April 1980).

Krippner, Stanley. "An Alternative to Drug Treatment for Hyperactive Children." *Academic Therapy*, Vol. 10, No. 4 (1975), pp. 433–439.

Kronick, Doreen. "Learning from Living: A Case History—Sugar, Fried Oysters and Zinc." *Academic Therapy*, Vol. 11, No. 1 (Fall 1975), pp. 119–121.

Laker, Martin. "On Determining Trace Element Levels in Man: The Uses of Blood and Hair." *The Lancet*, July 31, 1982.

Lansky, Vicki. *The Taming of the C.A.N.D.Y. Monster*. New York: Bantam Books, 1982.

Leboyer, Frederick. *Birth Without Violence*. New York: Alfred A. Knopf, 1975.

Leo, John. "Lessons in Bringing Up Baby." *Time*, October 22, 1984, p. 97.

Lesser, Michael, M.D. *Nutrition and Vitamin Therapy*. New York: Grove Press, 1980.

Levin, Alan S., M.D., and Merla Zellerbach. "Do You *Really* Have an Allergy?" *Prevention*, March 1984.

Levine, Melvin D., and Frank Oberklaid. "Hyperactivity: Symptom Complex or Complex Symptom." *American Journal of Disabled Children*, Vol. 134 (April 1980).

————, and Raun D. Melmed. "The Unhappy Wanderers: Children with Attention Deficits." Boston, MA: The Children's Hospital Medical Center.

Levinson, Harold N. *A Solution to the Riddle Dyslexia*. New York: Springer-Verlag, 1980.

Lilliston, Lynn. *Megavitamins: A New Key to Health*. New York: Fawcett, 1975.

Lindenbaum, E. S., and J. J. Mueller. "Effects of Pyridoxine on Mice after Immobilization Stress." *Journal of Nutrition and Metabolism*, Vol. 17 (1974), pp. 368–374.

Lynn, Roa, Neil D. Gluckin, and Bernard Kripke. *Learning Disabilities: An Overview of Theories, Approaches, and Politics*. New York: The Free Press, 1979.

Maugh, Thomas H., II. "Hair: A Diagnostic Tool to Complement Blood Serum and Urine." *Science,* Vol. 202 (December 22, 1978).

Michaelson, I. A., and M. W. Sauderhoff. "Lead Poisoning." *Medical World News,* September 7, 1973.

Mindell, Earl. *Vitamin Bible.* Los Angeles, CA: Cancer Control Society.

Montagu, Ashley. *Life Before Birth.* New York: New American Library, 1964.

National Information Center for Handicapped Children and Youth. "Learning Disabilities." A report, undated.

National Institute of Mental Health. "Why Is a Child Learning Disabled?" A report, undated.

————. "Plain Talk About Children with Learning Disabilities." A report, undated.

National Institutes of Health Consensus Development. "Defined Diets and Childhood Hyperactivity." Conference Summary, Vol. 4, No. 3.

Office of Children Development and Office of Assistant Secretary for Health and Scientific Affairs, Department of Health, Education and Welfare. "Good Anti-Stimulant Drug Arguments for Hyperactive Kids." From Report of Conference on Use of Stimulant Drugs, January 1971.

Osman, Betty B., and Henriette Blinder. *No One to Play With: The Social Side of Learning Disabilities.* New York: Random House, 1982.

Packard, Vance. *Our Endangered Children: Growing Up in a Changing World.* Boston, MA: Little, Brown, 1983.

Pasamanick, B., and A. A. Kawi. "Association of Factors of Pregnancy with Reading Disorders in Childhood." *Journal of the American Medical Association,* March 1968, pp. 1420–1423.

————, M. E. Rogers, and A. M. Lilienfeld. "Pregnancy Experience and Development of Behavior Disorders in Children." *American Journal of Psychiatry*, Vol. 112, (1956), pp. 613–618.

Passwater, Richard. *Supernutrition: Megavitamin Revolution.* New York: The Dial Press, 1975.

Pauling, Linus. "Orthomolecular Psychiatry." *Science*, Vol. 160, No. 3825 (April 19, 1968), pp. 265–271.

Pear, Robert. "Report Cites Drop in Prenatal Care." *The New York Times*, January 3, 1984.

Pechter, Kerry. "Should You Have Your Head Examined?" *Prevention*, January 1984.

Pfeiffer, C. C. *Mental and Elemental Nutrients.* New Canaan, CT: Keats Publishing, Inc., 1974.

————. "Observations on Trace and Toxic Elements in Hair and Serum." *Journal of Orthomolecular Psychiatry*, Vol. 3, No. 4 (1974), pp. 259–264.

Philips, Irving. "Research Directions in Child Psychiatry." *American Journal of Psychiatry*, Vol. 137, No. 11 (November 1980).

Powers, H.W.S., Jr. "Caffeine, Behavior, and the LD Child." *Academic Therapy*, Vol. 11, No. 1 (1975), pp. 5–11.

————. "Dietary Measures to Improve Behavior and Achievement." *Academic Therapy*, Vol. 9, No. 3 (1973), pp. 203–214.

Randolph, Theron G, and Ralph W. Moss. *An Alternative Approach to Allergies.* New York: Bantam Books, 1982.

Rapp, Doris J. "Does Diet Affect Hyperactivity?" *Journal of Learning Disabilities*, Vol. 11, No. 6 (June/July 1978).

Remsberg, Bonnie. "I Wisk I Culd Read and Writ." *Family Circle*, September 1981.

Renshaw, Domeena C. *The Hyperactive Child.* Boston, MA: Little, Brown, 1975.

Restak, Richard M. "An Autistic Idiot Savant." *Minneapolis Star and Tribune*, September 8, 1982.

Rimland, Bernard. "The Feingold Diet: An Assessment of the Reviews by Mattes, by Kavale and Forness and Others."

Journal of Learning Disabilities, Vol. 16, No. 6 (June/July 1983).

Rosner, Jerome. *Helping Children Overcome Learning Difficulties.* New York: Walker and Company, 1979.

Ross, Bette M. *Our Special Child: A Guide to Successful Parenting of Handicapped Children.* New York: Walker and Company, 1981.

Sabo, Ruth. "Trading in Additives for Tranquillity." *Prevention,* October 1977.

Salem News, The. March/April 1982, May 1982.

Sandoval, Jonathan, Nadine Lambert, and Dana M. Sassone. "The Comprehensive Treatment of Hyperactive Children: A Continuing Problem." *The Journal of Learning Disabilities,* Vol. 14, No. 3 (1981).

Saturday Review. "New Prospects for American Medicine." February 17, 1979.

Schauss, Alexander G. *Diet, Crime and Delinquency.* Berkeley, CA: Parker House, 1980.

Scherer, B., and W. Kramer. "Influence of Niacinamide Administration on Brain 5-HT and a Possible Mode of Action." *Life Science,* Vol. 1 (1972), pp. 189–195.

Simpson, Eileen. *Reversals: A Personal Account of Victory over Dyslexia.* Boston, MA: Houghton Mifflin, 1979.

Smith, Lendon. *Foods for Healthy Kids.* New York: McGraw-Hill, 1981.

Smith, Sally L. *No Easy Answers.* New York: Bantam Books, 1980.

Spock, Benjamin. *Baby and Child Care, rev. ed.* New York: Duell, Sloan & Pearce, 1965.

Stone, Thomas L. "Can Everyday Allergies Cause Mental Illness?" *Chicago Tribune,* January 23, 1980.

Stoutt, Glenn R., Jr. *The First Month of Life: A Parent's Guide to Care of the Newborn.* New York: Signet, 1981.

Swanson, James M., and Marcel Kinsbourne. "Should You Use Stimulants to Treat the Hyperactive Child?" *Modern Medicine*, April 15, 1978.

Tanne, Janice Hopkins. "Learning Disabilities—How to Help Your Child." *New York*, August 16, 1982.

"Talk of the Town, The." *The New Yorker*. June 27, 1983.

Tarnopol, Lester. *Learning Disorders in Children (Diagnosis, Medication, Education)*. Boston, MA: Little, Brown, 1971.

———, ed. *Learning Disorders in Children*. Proceedings of the World Federation of Neurology meeting in Dallas, Texas. Boston, MA: Little, Brown, 1968.

Weiss, Gabrielle, *et. al.* "Hyperactives as Young Adults: A Controlled Prospective Ten-Year Follow-up of 75 Children." *Archives of General Psychiatry*, Vol. 36 (June 1979).

———, and Lily Hechtman. "The Hyperactive Child Syndrome." *Science*, Vol. 205 (September 28, 1979).

Williams, R. J., J. D. Heffley, and C. W. Bode. "The Nutritive Value of Single Foods." Paper presented to the National Academy of Sciences, April 1971.

———, and Dwight K. Kalita. *A Physician's Handbook on Orthomolecular Medicine*. Elmsford, NY: Pergamon Press, 1977.

Wright, Jonathan V., M.D. "A Case of Allergy-Related Backache." *Prevention*, December 1983.

Wunderlich, R. C. "Treatment of the Hyperactive Child." *Academic Therapy*, Vol. 8, No. 4 (1973), pp. 375–390.

———. "Biosocial Factors in the Child with School Problems." *Academic Therapy*, Vol. 10, No. 4 (1975), pp. 389–399.

———. *Kids, Brains, & Learning*. St. Petersburg, FL: Johnny Reads, Inc., 1973.

———. *Allergy, Brains, & Children Coping*. St. Petersburg, FL: Johnny Reads, Inc., 1973.

Wurtman, R. J. "Nutrition and the Brain." *Journal of Food Technology*, March 1975.

Index

INDEX

Cushing, Harvey, M.D., 6
Cysteine, 40, 47, 50, 54
Cystic fibrosis, 37
Cytotoxic test, 104, 108–110

Degenerative diseases, 30
Developmental aphasia, 4
Diabetes, 41
Diagnosis, 51, 75, 154
Diet, 7, 27, 28, 30, 32, 33, 41, 42,
    48, 49, 52, 58, 59, 87, 88, 92,
    97, 98, 99, 104, 105, 106, 111,
    112, 114, 134, 136, 141, 170,
    199–218, 219
Dietary reform, 7, 91
Double-blind studies, 171
Down's syndrome, 26, 71, 84–87, 167
    case history
    Jonathan V., 86–87
Dropouts, school, 10
Drugs, 4, 6, 10, 21, 22, 23, 26, 49,
    92, 113, 114, 115, 127, 134,
    135, 137, 139, 164
Dyscalcula, 15
Dyschronia, 76
Dysgraphia, 15
Dyslexia, 4, 11, 14, 15, 56, 57, 149,
    150, 151

Earaches, 101, 103, 114
Earth Day, 164
Edison, Thomas, 6
EEG (electroencephalogram), 41, 43,
    170
Einstein, Albert, 6
Eliot, T. S., 138
Etzione, Amitai, 145

Family physician, 20, 36
Fatty acids, 31
Fetus, 133, 134, 135, 137
Finger control, 15
Flaubert, Gustave, 6
Fluoride, 141
Folic acid, 31, 51, 53, 120
Food and Drug Act, 164
Food and Drug Administration, 98

Foods, elimination of, 28, 33, 91, 95,
    96–97, 103, 104–106
Foundation for Nutrition and Stress
    Research, 93
Fraiberg, Selma, 140
Freud, Sigmund, and colleagues, 73
Freudian techniques, 20
Funk, Casimir, 113

Genetic origins, 13
Glucose tolerance test, 41, 42, 47, 96
Gordon, Garry F., M.D., 38
G.T.F. chromium, 50

Hair testing, 7, 35, 36, 37, 38, 40, 41,
    47, 54
Harrell, Dr. Ruth, 112
Harris, Sydney, 148
Harvard Medical School Health Letter,
    113–114
Health, Education, and Welfare, Dept.
    of, 22, 23
Hearing, 47, 82
Hearing disorders, 4, 42, 43
Hoffer, Abram, M.D., 24, 170–171
Honey, 219n
Huxley, Aldous, 30
Huxley, Sir Julian, 31
Hyperactivity, 3, 8, 12, 15, 21, 25, 26,
    33, 38, 41, 44, 54, 55, 56, 57,
    71, 72, 74, 95, 99, 102, 104,
    105, 124, 169, 170
Hyperkinetic, 14, 20, 23, 49
Hypertension, 141
Hypoglycemia, 30, 37, 56, 95–97

Iceland, 10
Industrial Revolution, 81, 142
Infant deaths, 137, 138, 139, 143
Inositol, 55, 120
Iodine, 209
IQ, 13, 85, 111, 112
Ireland, Glenn and Mallie, 87
Iron, 125, 141, 208
Iron deficiency, 36
Isoleucine, 55

Index

INDEX

INDEX

Vitamin D, 93, 103, 111, 115, 123, 141, 205
Vitamin E, 48, 50, 53, 54, 115, 123, 205
Vitamin K, 115, 124, 205
Vitamin P (the bioflavonoids), 124, 206
Vitamin syllabus, 115–124

WBD (wastebasket diagnosis), 75
Wheat, 33, 103, 214–215

Yeats, W. B., 6

Zinc, 37, 40, 41, 48, 115, 125, 127, 210
Zinc gluconate, 50

About the Authors

Allan Cott, M.D., of New York, is an orthomolecular physician in private practice and on the attending staff of Gracie Square Hospital. He is a Life Fellow of the American Psychiatric Association, a founding Fellow, a former President, and the present Chairman of the Board of the Academy of Orthomolecular Psychiatry. He is the consultant to the Allan Cott School for children with severe disorders of behavior, communication, and learning. He is the author of many articles on the treatment of mental illness in adults and on the treatment of seriously disturbed children and learning disabled children with vitamins, minerals, and dietary control. He has lectured extensively throughout the United States and in many other countries. He was the recipient in 1982 of the Dixie Annette Award for distinguished services as physician, teacher, humanist, and pioneer in orthomolecular psychiatry. (The award is granted yearly by the Huxley Institute for Biosocial Research.) He has been honored by the National Society for Autistic Children and by the Child Mental Health Services, of Birmingham, Alabama. He is the author of two best-sellers, *Fasting: The Ultimate Diet* and *Fasting as a Way of Life*.

Jerome Agel and Eugene Boe, of New York, were co-authors with Dr. Cott of the best-sellers *Fasting: The Ultimate Diet* and *Fasting as a Way of Life*. They have written many other books together, including the novels *22 Fires* and *Deliverance in Shanghai*.